REVELATION
A Love Letter From God

Katheryn Maddox Haddad

Other Books by this Author

TOPICAL
Applied Christianity: Handbook 500 Good Works
Christianity or Islam? The Contrast
The Holy Spirit: 592 Verses Examined
The Road to Heaven
Love Letters of Jesus & His Bride, Ecclesia
The Best of Alexander Campbell & His Millennial Harbinger
Inside the Hearts of Bible Women-Reader+Audio+Leader
Revelation: A Love Letter From God
Worship Changes Since 1st Century + Worship 1sr Century Way
Was Jesus God? (Why Evil)
365 Life-Changing Scriptures Day by Date
The Road to Heaven
The Lord's Supper: 52 Readings with Prayers

FUN BOOKS
Bible Puzzles, Bible Song Book, Bible Numbers

TOUCHING GOD SERIES
365 Golden Bible Thoughts: God's Heart to Yours
365 Pearls of Wisdom: God's Soul to Yours
365 Silver-Winged Prayers: Your Spirit to God's

-SURVEY SERIES: EASY BIBLE WORKBOOKS
→Old Testament & New Testament Surveys
→Questions You Have Asked-Parts I & II

HISTORICAL RESEARCH BIBLE
for Novel, Screenwriter, Documentary & Thesis Writers

HISTORICAL NOVELS & STORYBOOKS
Series of 8: They Met Jesus
Ongoing Series of 8: Intrepid Men of God
Mysteries of the Empire with Klaudius & Hektor
Christmas: They Rocked the Cradle that Rocked the World
Series of 8: A Child's Life of Christ
Series of 10: A Child's Bible Heroes
Series of 8: A Child's Bible Kids
Series of 10: A Child's Bible Ladies

Genealogy: How to Climb Your Family Tree Without Falling Out
Volume I & 2: Beginner-Intermediate & Colonial-Medieval

Copyright ⓒ 2014 Katheryn Maddox Haddad
Northern Lights Publishing House
ISBN 978-1-948462-96-9

Scripture taken from the HOLY BIBLE, NEW INTERNATIONAL VERSION. Copyright 19673, 1978, 1984 International Bible Society. Used by permission of Zondervan Bible Publishers.
Printed in the United States

In Praise of
Revelation: A Love Letter from God

* * * * Refreshing Take on book of Revelation – E. Coughlin So glad to see a book written about Revelation that **celebrates** and glorifies the center of it all and the reason for the book: our great and glorious Savior, Jesus!

* * * * * In Depth – AMAZON CUSTOMER The depth of the author's knowledge of Revelation along with her ability to convey God's message of love to us is **incredible.** This book unlocks the mysteries of the book of Revelation. If you want to better understand the book of Revelation, this is a must read book!

* * * * **– Good insight. ANONYMOUS.** This is a very interesting interpretation of Revelation It offers good **insight**.

* * * * * Amazed – CRWAL - To say the very least, I am simply amazed by the author's knowledge of the book and her ability to make it **understandable to the ordinary person.** I have struggled for years to understand all the numbers and symbols, but thankfully, with the author's help, it is much **clearer.** Katheryn Haddad is a gifted writer and I personally want to thank her for sharing her gift from God in such a **wonderful** way.

* * * * * – A MUST READ – AMAZON CUSTOMER. A MUST READ!!

* * * * **– Interesting – Harold Maxwell -** Interesting

***** – A Must Read – Destanie Jean
If you have a hard time reading revelations this book will help you **understand what it's talking about!** Love it. A **great** study!!!

An Encouraging Word for You

Revelation is not a book of gloom and doom. It is a book of hope. A book of reassurance that, no matter how bad things get in the world, God is still in control and still loves us like light shimmering in the soul.

It was written during a time when Christians were losing jobs and homes, friends and family. During a time when Christians were being imprisoned, tortured, and killed. They were laying everything on the line for Jesus. Everything! They needed hope. They needed this love letter.

This is a history of the ancient world before Jesus was born, especially the world of the Israelites. It is also an account of Jesus birth, ministry, and death. It ends with the final doom of Satan and the final victory of the church, the heavenly Jerusalem. After all, does not chapter 1, verse 19 state that John was to "write, therefore, what you have seen [past], what is now [present], and what will take place later [future]"?

The scriptures always interpret themselves; therefore, the author takes you through each scene with applicable background scriptures to magnify the meaning with unique clearness.

This is God's last love letter to the world. He has done everything possible to help us escape hell, including offering his only begotten son to die in our place. We are his children. He loves us and does not want us to be hurt. He tells of the overwhelming joy he can give those who accept his Son as Lord of their life. He also tells us that, if we become Christians, he will protect us as he always protected his children in the past. This is one last reassure. One last love letter from God.

Cast aside all the horror stories you have been told about Revelation. View it now with fresh new eyes, be awed, and be showered with God's love.

Table of Contents

(The epistles in Chapters 1-3 are not covered in this book)

Other Books by this Author ii
In Praise of Revelation: A Love Letter from God iii

An Encouraging Word for You iv
Brief Outline of Revelation vi

Chapter 4. God's Throne Room 1
Chapter 5. Jesus is Introduced 6
Chapter 6. Six Seals of Sin In the Book of History 12
Chapter 7. Seventh (Final) Seal is Salvation 19
Chapter 8. Seven Trumpets of Historic Reminders ~ God
         the Punishers 26
Chapter 9. Seven Trumpets of Historic Reminders ~ Israelites
         Chastised 31
Chapter 10. Seven Thunders of Judgment; 38
         Day of Judgment Postponed 38
Chapter 11. Predictions and Preview of the Life of Christ 42
Chapter 12. Jesus' Birth & The Birth of Christianity…........... 48
Chapter 13. …At a Time of God-Kings & Paganism
         as Predicted 53
Chapter 14. Jesus' Ministry on Earth 61
Chapter 15. Jesus' Triumphal Entry Into Jerusalem 69
Chapter 16. Jesus, the Lamb of God, Pours Out His Blood 73
Chapter 17. Earthly Kingdoms & Paganism Now Lose
         their Power 79
Chapter 18. Rejoice! The Overcoming Church Is
         Almost Here 86
Chapter 19. The Bride of Christ Gets Ready for Her
         Wedding 92
Chapter 20. Satan Loses His Power 99
Chapter 21. Now the Victorious Church Begins…................. 104
Chapter 22. Faithful Until the Groom Comes for the

Wedding in Heaven 111

SYNOPSES OF EACH CHAPTER..118
JEWISH SYMBOLIC MEANING OF NUMBERS**Error! Bookmark not defined.**

Thank You 131
About the Author...132

Buy Your Next Book Now 133
Connect With The Author...134

Get A Free Book..134
Join My Dream Team 134

Brief Outline of Revelation

Chap. 1-3:	Greetings
Chap. 4-5:	Master Plan to Save Mankind
Chap. 6-7:	Seven Seals of Sin & Salvation
Chap. 8-9:	Six Trumpets of Historic Reminders ~ Victories in Old Testament Era
Chap. 10-11:	Seven Warning Thunders Within the 6th Trumpet
Chap. 12-15:	Seventh Trumpet of Historic Reminders ~ Victories in the New Testament Era
Chap. 16-19:	Seven Cups of Wrath ~ Jesus Battles Against Sin
Chap. 20:	Seventh Trumpet of Final Victory ~ All Fulfilled as Promised From the Beginning
Chap. 21:	Victorious Reign of the Church Forever

Chapter 4. God's Throne Room

Verses 1-4

John's vision opens with promise. With glory. With the verdant throne of the very Creator of the universe. And the One who loves us beyond words, beyond thoughts, beyond imaginations.

God is depicted as being jasper, which is sometimes red, sometimes yellow, sometimes green. A God who is ever changing ~ adapting ~ as our needs change, but never changing (James 1:17). Jasper is usually red, and it reminds us of the blood of Jesus shed in our place.

Surrounding the throne is a rainbow, an aura of emerald. Does it represent earth? Is God in the midst of us as we search for him? Emerald is usually translated from a word meaning fresh. God never tires. He continually watches us as a parent for his children. Always caring for us. Always listening for us.

Remember, Revelation is full of symbolism. So, who are the twenty-four elders? They are twice twelve. Two represents strength. Twelve dominates the scriptures; specifically, the twelve tribes of Israel (Exodus 39:14), and Jesus' twelve apostles (Matthew 10:2). (See the number symbolism chart in the back). They represent the saved of the Old Testament plus the saved of the New Testament.

They are dressed in white. The Psalmist said, "purge me...Wash me and I shall be whiter than snow" (51:7), and the prophet said, "Though your sins be as scarlet, they shall be as white as snow" (Isaiah 1:18). So these twenty-four elders have had their sins all forgiven, and are now pure before God.

They wear crowns of gold. I Corinthians 9:25 refers to our imperishable crown, Philippians 4:1 to a crown of joy, I Thessalonians 2:19 to a crown of rejoicing, II Timothy 4:8 to a crown of righteousness, James 1:12 to a crown of life, and I Peter 5:4 to a crown of glory. What amazing crowns they have.

Further, the crowns are made of gold. They were purged of their sins like gold, with all impurities gone (Malachi 3:3). Now, having been tested as gold, they call out God's name, and he answers (Zechariah 13:9b).

Interestingly, I Corinthians 4:8 says we Christians reign as kings right now, and II Timothy 2:12 says we shall reign with Christ. Since all Christians reign right now and will reign later, these twenty-four elders are representatives of all God's people, both in the Old Testament era and the New Testament era.

Verse 5

From the throne we hear thunderings, rumblings, and flashes of lightning. God is a living, vibrant and dynamic God whose work is never done. He reigns supreme. He is electrifying. He is power unquenchable ~ the power of love that is ever protecting his children and never stopping to rest.

Before his throne are seven lamps, seven signifying 4 + 3. We have the four corners of the earth and the four winds, all representing earth. We have God the Father, God the Son, God the Spirit, representing heaven.

In the Jewish religion, there were seven lamps on one lampstand (Exodus 25:31, 27), and it stood in the Holy Place outside the curtain leading to the Most Holy Place to spread its light from evening to morning (Leviticus 24:3).

When an angel appeared to prophet Zechariah, he had with him such a lampstand, and the prophet asked what it represented. The angel replied, "This is the word of the Lord to Zerubbabel: 'Not by might or by power, but by my Spirit,' says the Lord Almighty" (Zechariah 4:2-6). So, symbolically, the lampstand represents the power of the Holy Spirit. But it also represents a "lamp to my feet and a light to my path" (Psalm 119:105).

What about the fire in the seven lamps? They have meaning too. One prophet said it represented the eyes of the Lord (Zechariah 5:10). Another said it represented the refiner's fire to purify us as gold unto righteousness (Malachi 3:2-3), as also noted by Paul in I Corinthians 3:13.

Another prophet said fire represents the Word of God (Jeremiah 20:9). The Word of God always refines us, revealing our heart as we respond or fail to respond to it. We see this later when tongues of fire descended on the twelve apostles and they began to speak the Word of God in other languages.

So now we see that the light of these seven lamps glow throughout heaven and illuminate the earth to light our path. It also refines us and makes us pure, then illuminates our path to spread God's heavenly Word throughout the earth. God loves us so. He wants to give us every advantage, including the light of his Word to get us through this hard life.

Verse 6

To Christians, this is the sea of the spiritually dead from among all nations. Daniel 7:3 refers to four beasts coming out of the sea, and Revelation 20:13 says the spiritually dead will come up out of the sea. What is the significance?

The Red Sea was both a sea of life and of death. The Egyptians chasing the Israelites to bring them back to their slavery drowned in that sea. But the Israelites walked to the other side, free of their slavery forever. I Corinthians 10:1-2 says they were baptized unto Moses, with the cloud over their heads and the waters on each side of them. Romans 6:3-4 says in baptism, we die, then come back to life, our souls born again.

On the throne of God are four living creatures. Four represents earth. They have eyes that can see everywhere. They have wings and wheels full of eyes that take them everywhere. And they have four faces.

Verse 7

Who were the four living creatures? There are four passages in the Bible that mention them or creatures close to them.

Isaiah 6:1-7 identifies them as **seraphim** with six wings above the throne of God.

Ezekiel 1:5-28 identifies them as being under the firmament, with the appearance of a rainbow, with sapphire thrones above their heads. They moved around in wheels, the wheels were full of eyes and their spirit was in the wheels. They had four faces ~ one of a man, one of a lion, one of an ox, and one of an eagle.

Ezekiel 10:1, 22 identifies them as **cherubim** being high under the firmament with a sapphire throne. They were in the south side of the temple, they moved around with wheels full of eyes, and had four faces. They had four wings, and their wings were full of eyes also.

Revelation 4:2-8 says they were full of eyes and had six wings full of eyes. As with Ezekiel, they had faces of a lion, a calf, a man, and an eagle. But, here, they are in the middle of God's throne, and they are always saying, "Holy! Holy! Holy, Lord God Almighty!"

In the first three instances, they are above the throne of God, and in the last (Revelation), they are on God's throne.

Their wings have eyes and the wheels they travel in are full of eyes, both meaning they can travel everywhere and see everything. What about their four faces?

One is the face of a lion. Genesis 49:8-10 predicts that out of the tribe of Judah will come a lion king. In John 18:37 Jesus said he was a king.

One is the face of a calf or oxen. They were offered for forgiveness of sins (Leviticus 8:14-15). In Hebrews 4:14-15, Jesus is named as our high priest who offered himself (Hebrews 9:13-14). Jesus was the calf/oxen.

One was the face of an eagle. Proverbs 23:5 talks about an eagle flying up into the sky between heaven and earth. I Timothy 2:5 says Jesus is the mediator between heaven and earth. Jesus was the eagle.

One was the face of a man. Jesus called himself the Son of Man" (Matthew 9:6), also interpreted as the Son of Mankind. Hebrews 10:4-6 says he got a body so he could die. Jesus was the man.

Therefore, it can be concluded that these four living creatures, formerly above the throne of God, and now on the throne of God, but traveling anywhere, are the Spirit of Jesus in heaven and on earth.

Verses 8-11

Continually day and night, the Spirit of Jesus cries out from the throne of God, "Holy is the Lord God Almighty". Just before Jesus' death, Jesus cried out for God to glorify his name, and God replied in the thunder, "I have glorified it and I will glorify it" (John 12:28-29).

The twenty-four elders leave their thrones, take off their crowns, and lay them at the foot of the throne, and utter

You are worthy, our Lord and God,
To receive glory and honor and power,
For you created all things,
And by your will they were created
And have their being.

Chapter 5. Jesus is Introduced

Verse 1

God is holding a scroll with seven seals keeping it closed. What are the seals?

Seal as a noun (*sephragis* in Greek) represents righteousness (Romans 4:11), and salvation (II Timothy 2:19).

Seal as a verb (*sphragizo* in Greek) is a little broader, but all pointing to seal as a noun. Jesus, who had seen God, set his seal that God is true (John 3:33), and said God places his seal of approval on believers (John 6:27). Paul sealed the Roman Christians with blessings of being Christians (Romans 15:28), and said God sealed his ownership to Christians with his Spirit in their hearts as a deposit guaranteeing their salvation (II Corinthians 1:22). The Ephesian Christians were told that those who hear and believe are sealed with the Holy Spirit as a deposit, guaranteeing their salvation (Ephesians 1:13), and were sealed with the Holy Spirit until the day of redemption (Ephesians 4:30).

So, even though some readers of Revelation interpret the seals as being bad things, they are interpreted here as being good ~ identifying the saved through the power of the Holy Spirit.

There is also the seal of God. Revelation 5:1-7 refers to the seven seals of sin and salvation on the book given to the Lamb (the same as being held by God in this chapter). Chapter 6 tells of six of the seals of sin being opened as punishment on people who just are not able to be sinless, as hard as they try.

But the seventh seal is completely different. The first six seals reveal that no one is sinless, no matter who they are. The seventh seal is the seal of God and is the seal of salvation (Revelation 7:2-3). When it is finally opened, everyone is dumbfounded (Revelation 8:1-6). More on this later.

Verses 2-3

Now there is an angel flying around heaven ~ not just an angel, a mighty angel ~ asking "Who is worthy to break the seals and open the scroll (the book)?" Sometimes angels do not have all the answers. In referring to the many prophecies of Jesus and the new and eternal kingdom of God, Peter not only said the prophets themselves didn't always understand what they were writing, but "Even angels long to look into these things" (I Peter 1:12).

Paul in Ephesians 3 talks about "the mystery". The mystery, when all scriptures using this word are investigated, is salvation. In verses 10 and 11 Paul says, "His intent was that now, through the church, the manifold wisdom of God should be made known to the rulers and authorities in the heavenly realms, according to his eternal purpose which he accomplished in Christ Jesus our Lord."

Remember, six of the seals are seals of sin, but the seventh is the seal of salvation. But at this point, the seals have not been opened. Finally, it is concluded that no one in heaven or on earth is able to open the scroll/book and see what is written in it.

Verses 4-5

John weeps because no one has been found worthy to open the seals and read the book. The word "worthy" here is from the Greek *axios*, meaning to earn the right. God is holding the book. It is obviously the Words of God. John wants to know what God has to say.

But the twenty-four elders know the secret, and one of them shares it with John: Jesus has won the victory, so is able to open the seven seals and reveal what is in the book.

After all, Jesus is the Lion of Judah with the scepter (Genesis 49:9-10). That branch from Jesse (Isaiah 11:1-3), the descendant of King David, is a heavenly king (Matthew 1:3-6, 17). He has triumphed, he has prevailed over evil. He it is who was strong enough to make salvation possible.

Interestingly, the word for "open" is *anoigo*, meaning to reopen. This is going to be a retelling of mankind's history and ever-losing struggle to be sinless.

Verses 6-7

John has looked away from the throne of God a moment to confer with the elder, possibly one of his old friends among the original twelve apostles who followed Jesus everywhere.

Now he looks back at the throne and it is different. For now, Jesus is standing on the throne looking like a lamb and all bloody. Is that what the elder meant by triumphant? Indeed, it is. The Lamb may be bloody, but the Lamb came out of the battle victorious.

Around Jesus are the four living creatures. Remember, they represent the Spirit of Jesus.

The Lamb has seven horns. There were horns at the corners of the Jewish altar of incense (later in Revelation the smoke from the incense is described as the prayers of the saints), and on the corners of the altar of burnt offerings for our sins. (Exodus 37:25; 38:1-2).

God is called the "horn of my salvation" in II Samuel 22:3; Psalm 18:2; and Luke 1:67-69. Horns represent kingship in Psalm 132:1-18 and Daniel 7:7, 23-24.

Why seven horns? Seven comes from three (heavenly) plus four (earthly). Although bloody, Jesus is depicted as the valiant warrior king of both heaven and earth.

Jesus, the Lamb, also has seven eyes, being the Spirit of God that is everywhere, in heaven and on earth. Jesus was full of the Spirit after his baptism and temptation (Luke 4:14). He had the Spirit without measure (John 3:34). He was the Spirit of Truth that returned to earth after Jesus ascended to heaven (John 14:16-17; 16:7; 17:17). In fact, Paul refers to the Spirit of Jesus Christ (Philippians 1:19).

The bloody but victorious Lamb takes the book from the right hand of he who is sitting on the throne. We will discuss the scroll/book in more detail later.

Verse 8

Whereas the twenty-four elders had been worshiping God sitting on the throne, they now worship the bloody Lamb-King standing in the middle of the throne. Remember Jesus is part of God. John 1:1 says "In the beginning was the Word, the Word was with God, and the Word was God" and verse 14 says the Word became flesh. Later on, the Word is called the Lamb of God (John 1:29).

Keep remembering that this book is full of symbolism. Symbolism is used to convey deep thoughts and ideas that cannot be conveyed in just a few words.

The four living creatures (the Spirit of Christ, subject to the will of Christ) and the twenty-four elders fall down before the bloody, triumphant warrior Lamb holding harps and golden bowls of incense. How can someone get down on his knees and then bow with his head to the floor while holding a harp and a bowl? They are symbolic! The verse itself says the bowls of incense represent the prayers of the saints. If they are symbolic, the harps are too. We find harps in Ephesians 5:19 referring to singing, and playing on the strings of our heart. So, what they are offering to Jesus are their prayers and their hearts.

Verses 9-10

The word "purchased" is from the Greek *agoraso*, meaning to buy at the forum or market. Mankind was up for sale to the highest bidder. Jesus paid the highest price, for he paid with his blood.

Now we reign, for the kingdom is the church (Colossians 1:13,18) which Jesus said would come in the lifetime of his hearers (Matthew 16:28). Now we are priests who offer our bodies as living human sacrifices (Romans 12:1) and offer the sacrifice of praise, the fruit of our lips (Hebrews 13:15).

The elders and our living creatures cannot hold back any longer. Everyone is ecstatically relieved that they will no longer have to go to hell. Everyone is so full of joy, they burst out in song. *You are worthy!* Yes, you, Lord Jesus. You are our hero. *To take the scroll of salvation and open the seals* blocking the way to it. *Because you were slain!* How could you do that, Lord Jesus? For me? For me.

With your blood you purchased men for God. The price. It was too much. But that is what Satan demanded. The penalty for sin is death. You actually paid it, Lord Jesus. *From every tribe and language and people and nation.* No one left out because of what or who they are. Such love. We don't understand that kind of love. It swells our souls in wonder.

You have made them to be a kingdom and priests to serve our God. We're already in the kingdom? Just like that? And we're our own priests? *And they will reign on the earth.* And, yes, we're reigning right now because the earth is right now. Christians are the elite in the spirit world. Christians reign because we are strong, and will only grow stronger. Lord Jesus, Lamb of God, accept our song.

Verses 11-12

It is catching! For now, the angels want in on the celebration. Ten thousand times ten thousand times ten thousand of them. All-inclusiveness times all-inclusiveness times all-inclusiveness (see the chart on numbers). All the angels, with no one left out. burst forth in their own song. But, whereas Jesus' followers sang to Jesus, the angels sing about Jesus.

Worthy is the Lamb who was slain. Not only the hero of all who were saved, but the hero of angels. God, the Word, actually became human in order to save humans. *To receive power! And wealth! And wisdom! And strength!* Power of the miraculous. Wealth of the universe. Wisdom of the ages. Strength beyond comprehension to have done what he did ~ stay on the cross to the end.

And honor! And glory! And praise! The highest of allegiance. The greatest of goodness. Praise that can never be given too much or too often.

Verses 13-14

Then the whole world joins in the song! The universe bursts forth in singing ~ every creature in heaven, on the earth, under the earth, and in the sea ~ everyone without exception, even those who never believed before. Even those who hate Jesus. The reality of what he did for us cannot be hidden. It must be declared, even by those who hate.

And so the whole earth, too, joins in: *To him who sits on the throne and to the Lamb!* Yes, to the one you despised and turned against because you were having too much fun making Satan your god. *Be praise!* Yes, now is the time to acknowledge Jesus after all. *And honor!* Now is the time to put him on the pedestal of your life where he had always belonged. *And glory!* The goodness you always looked down upon. *And power!* Goodness that formerly was considered weakness wasn't weak after all, for it prevailed over evil. *Forever and ever!*

A quiet and awestricken amen.

Now it is back to the four living creatures and the twenty-four elders, representing the saved. And once again they fall down and worship because they cannot get enough of worshiping their Savior, their God.

Chapter 6. Six Seals of Sin In the Book of History

First, just what is the "scroll" that the seals are keeping us from reading? The word in Hebrew is *sepher*, and in Greek is *biblos*.

Books in the Old Testament refer to civil matters such as genealogies (Genesis 5:1), or to the Law of Moses (Exodus 24:7; Deuteronomy 31:26; Galatians 3:10), or to books of prophecy. In the New Testament, books refer to the writings on Jesus' life and works (John 20:30), and the writings of Paul (II Timothy 4:13).

What about books (yes, there are more than one) in heaven? They refer to God's book (Exodus 32:32-33), the book of those who obey God (Psalm 40:7-8), the book of God's tears (Psalm 56:8), the book of life (Psalm 69:28), God's book (Psalm 139:16), books (Daniel 7:9-10), book of remembrance of those who honor God (Malachi 3:16); book of life (Philippians 4:3), book of life (Revelation 3:5), a little book of judgment (Revelation 10:2), the book of sinners not listed in the little book of life (Revelation 17:8), the book of the works of the spiritually dead (Revelation 20:12), the book of sinners not listed in the little book of life (Revelation 20:15), and the saved listed in the little book of life (Revelation 21:27).

What can we conclude about the books? There are three kinds. (1) The book of life contains the list of the saved of both the Old Testament and New Testament eras. (2) Individual books of lives contain events in each of our lives on earth. (3) The book of the spiritually dead, containing the works of unsaved sinners either by nation or individually. The book that the seven seals guard is the book of life, which can also be called the book of salvation.

SEAL ONE

Verses 1-2

The time for talk is over. Now is the time for action. The

Lamb steps forward and takes the first seal. The four living creatures (the essence of Christ's Spirit) thunder out their command: Come!

Suddenly John sees a white horse with a rider holding a bow, being given a crown, then riding out to conquer.

The word "white" in Greek is *leukos* from which the word leukemia comes. But, whereas there are too many white blood cells for the red to handle, thus causing serious illness, in this story, the white "cells" are too many for evil to handle. The significance of the white is that it represents those who are purged, washed, and cleansed of their sin (Psalm 51:7); those who have been refined, purified, and are not wicked (Daniel 12:10).

The "bow" referred to is *toxon* in Greek, referring to deadly poison. The bow shoots poison arrows, ready to kill sin and death.

The crown, as defined in the New Testament is the crown of rejoicing (I Thessalonians 2:19), the crown of righteousness (II Timothy 4:8), the crown of life (James 1:12), the crown of glory (I Peter 5:4).

The rider sets out to conquer, to "overcome" (Greek *nikao*) ~ overcome the world (John 16:33), overcome evil (Romans 12:21), overcome the wicked one, Satan (I John 2:13). And who is the rider? Chapter 19 says the rider is Faithful and True, dressed in a robe dipped in blood, and he is the Word of God ~ Jesus.

SEAL TWO

Verses 3-4

The white horse is followed by horses representing three forms of disaster on earth ~ war, famine, and plague.

The red horse represents war. "Red" in Greek is *purrhos*, referring to a Greek king who won a victory, but at the cost of much bloodshed. It is a fiery, bloody red. It is used in Numbers 21:6 in referring to the fiery, deadly serpents.

We will see later that the sword/war will be represented by the Israelites being captured by cruel Assyria (II Kings 17:5-6). The Assyrians were great warriors. Assyria was the most vicious of all nations. Their very name became a byword for cruelty. They skinned their prisoners alive and cut off various body parts to strike terror in their enemies. There are records of Assyrian officials pulling out tongues and displaying mounds of human skulls in order to terrify nearby nations into paying tribute to them from their wealth. The Assyrian king personally put out the eyes of all enemy kings, and led officials into captivity with hooks in their lips. Assyria was a world empire for about 300 years, and their war chronicles are more bloody than any other nation on earth.

The northern kingdom of Israel tried to get it right, but they couldn't do it. They couldn't be sinless. They continued to sin, and were punished by the Assyrians. They just couldn't get it right. They couldn't be sinless. They continued to sin more and more. But someday, Jesus' blood will redeem the righteous among them (Hebrews 9:15) from Satan's hold.

SEAL THREE

Verses 5-6

The black horse represents famine. "Black" in Greek is *melas*, the root word for malaise or depression. Lamentations 4:8-9 refers to black skin clinging to the bones as the person dies of hunger, and black skin hot with fever as a result of famine.

The rider has a pair of scales, and the announcement is made that a quart of wheat is selling for a denarius. Matthew 20:2 says a denarius is one day's wages. Obviously, this announcement is made about a famine. Jeremiah 19:9 says that, during a siege of Jerusalem when the gates were closed securely for years, people began eating the flesh of children and "friends". II Kings 25:1, 21 says the starving people of Judah were finally captured by the Babylonians.

So, just like the northern kingdom, the southern kingdom of Judah tried to get it right. They couldn't be sinless either. They continued to sin more and more. But someday, Jesus' blood will redeem the righteous among them (Romans 4:25) from Satan's hold.

SEAL FOUR

Verses 7-8

Now the pale horse. It represents plague. "Pale" in Greek is actually *chlorus* from which the word cholera came. Translated literally, it is mildew and mold. Leviticus 13:49 refers to the greenish or reddish plague in leather. Leviticus 14:36-37 refers to the greenish or reddish plague in walls. Haggai 2:17 said everything they grew was struck with blight and mildew. The word was used in Jeremiah 19:8, predicting Jerusalem will be full of plagues, in 49:17 where Edom will be full of plagues, and 50:13 where Babylon will be full of plagues.

Death sits on that pale horse. So, just as the Jews tried to get it right, so too, the pagan nations did. But they couldn't be sinless either. They continued to sin more and more. Jesus on the white horse was still in the lead, and someday Jesus' blood will redeem the righteous among them.

Hades, the grave, follows close behind the pale rider, accepting into its realm all those who were killed by war, hunger and plague. They were given power over part of the earth (see the chart on numbers).

SEAL FIVE

Verses 9-11

John is always told to look at each of the first four seals. He must not have wanted to look at them. It has just been a reminder that no one in the world can get it right; no one can be sinless. But this fifth seal must have stolen his heart, for it is the voice of martyred prophets.

Hebrews 11:32-40 refers to prophets who "faced jeers and

flogging, while still others were chained and put in prison. They were stoned; they were sawed in two; they were put to death by the sword. They went about in sheepskins and goatskins, destitute, persecute and mistreated. The world was not worthy of them. They wandered in deserts and mountains and in caves and holes in the ground."

And now they wait, crying out, "How long? How long?". They are given white robes of sinlessness and told to wait for others to be converted and martyred. It is still going on today. We have Christian brothers and sisters who are being persecuted worldwide by losing their jobs, their homes, and sometimes their families. We have Christian brothers and sisters in the Far East and Middle East who are being hauled off to prison, tortured, and finally executed as traitors.

But Jesus is still on his white horse and he is still leading. Some day Jesus' blood will redeem the righteous from the blackness of sin and Satan and give them white robes of sinlessness.

SEAL SIX

Verses 12-14

Yes, Jesus is still in the lead. He has tried to lead mankind, and though they follow to some degree, they all have their own agendas. Jesus has led mankind through all the times that the Israelites and pagans tried to be sinless their own way, and all failed. Instead, all they accomplished was war, famine and plague, almost all of which is the result of sin. Now we look again at the one on the white horse, the one covered with blood. Now, he is ready to rescue them all. And us.

There is a great earthquake. What happened at Jesus' crucifixion? Matthew 27:51-52 says the earth shook so hard, tombs were laid open, and the curtain guarding the Most Holy Place in the temple tore in half. Further, in verse 45, it tells how the sun turned black, representing the blackness of our sins. When the moon shines through dark clouds during the day such as an eclipse, it has a reddish hue, and in this case it represented blood ~ the bloodshed during mankind's darkest hour.

Periodically, Satan has visited heaven and been kicked out. Remember Job chapter 1? Remember when Jesus sent out the 72 evangelists and they returned with success stories of receptive hearts. Remember how Jesus declared with joy that he was watching Satan fall (Luke 10:18)?

Now, for the final fall where Satan can never rise again. Now for the victory. Now for the crowning moment. Now Satan falls forever. Now, although Jesus has been wounded in his heal temporarily, Satan has been crushed in his head (Genesis 3:15). So, it is with confidence that Paul says each of us since then has our own chance to crush Satan and put him under our own feet (Romans 16:20).

Now is the Day of the Lord (Joel 2:10). Now is the Day of Decision (Joel 3:14-16). Now is fulfilled what had been prophesied so many centuries earlier: The Day Jesus brings Satan down (Obadiah 2-4).

What a Day! The day Christians look forward to. The day we are allowed entry into our heavenly home.

Verses 15-17

But it is the day unbelievers dread. For when the heavens open like a scroll and Jesus descends to take us back to heaven with him (I Thessalonians 4:16-17), unbelievers, those who refuse Jesus in their life, will try unsuccessfully to hide from God ~ presidents, prime ministers, members of parliament, congressmen, governors, mayors, CEOs, financial gurus, dukes, earls, economic barons, Wall Street wizards, sports heroes, movie stars as well as garbage collectors, ditch diggers, water carriers, slaves, prostitutes, maids, butlers, waitresses, dishwashers, persecutors of Christian friends, persecutors of politically opposing Christians, persecutors of Christians who made everyone else look bad.

If they spend their life running from Jesus, they will now make one last run. Deep down those who are among them know.

They have always known. They are not going to get by with lying, cheating, envying, and every other "harmless" thing they have done any more. They can run, but they cannot hide. Adam tried it, and it did not work (Genesis 3:8-11). It never works to hide from God.

And so, all those who thought Jesus and his followers are weak, come to terms with their wrong assumptions borne out of hard hearts who wanted to do everything Satan's way. Now they see that Jesus is not only a Lamb, but he is a Lion.

Chapter 7. Seventh (Final) Seal is Salvation

The seventh seal starts the history all over again. We go back now, to the Old Testament era.

Verse 1-2

There are four angels standing on the four corners of the earth, holding back the four winds of the earth (see the chart on numbers). They stand guard over the earth until the Christians can be rescued from the earth. Yes, God watches out for his own.

A fifth angel comes from the east having the seal of God, the seventh seal. Why the east?

The entrance to the Garden of Eden was in the east (Genesis 3:24). The ruler over kings, the first and the last, came from the east (Isaiah 41:2-4). The glory of God came into the new temple through the east gate, and was closed after that because God entered through it; although it was opened on the Sabbath (Ezekiel 43:1-4; 44:1-2; 46:1). The altar in the temple faced east (Ezekiel 43:17), the prince/king of the Jews sat at the east gate, and he made voluntary burnt offerings at the east gate (Ezekiel 46:12). The front entrance of the temple itself faced east (Ezekiel 47:1).

Verse 3

Now "seal" is turned from a noun/name to an action verb. The earth is not to be destroyed by the angels until the seal of salvation is put on the foreheads of the servants of God. Who are the servants of God? The Israelites whose sins have been blotted out; the redeemed (Isaiah 44:21-22). Later the servants of God will be Christians who have been baptized "unto a new life" (Romans 6:3-4, 22).

What do the foreheads represent? Exodus 28:36-38 refers to a signet plate upon which is written "holiness to the Lord". It was a declaration worn by the high priest. All Christians are priests, and figuratively bear this on our forehead.

Forehead is next mentioned when David slew Goliath by

slinging a rock into his forehead (I Samuel 17:49). The forehead protects the brain unless someone knows how to break through it as David did. II Chronicles 26:19-20 says leprosy broke out on King Uzziah's forehead and horrified everyone who saw it. The forehead is a part of the body usually not clothed or hidden. It helps to identify a person. In the case of Christians, it identifies what we are.

Jeremiah 3:3 refers to a prostitute's forehead that does not blush, is not ashamed, but is stubborn. Ezekiel 3:8-9 says strong-willed people butt heads (foreheads) with other people and refuse to be afraid or dismayed. Finally, Ezekiel 9:4 refers to putting a mark on the foreheads of men who are intensely discouraged over the terrible things that have happened within Jerusalem (eating their own children, etc. as mentioned above). This refers to Christians who are stubborn, strong, and intense in our discouragement with sin, and belief in God.

Revelation refers to the seal of God being on the foreheads of God's servants (7:3), are not to be harmed (9:4), are people with God the Father's name on their forehead (14:1), Christian martyrs (20:4), and those beholding God's face (22:4).

Satan has a seal too. It is referred to in Revelation as the mark of the beast (13:16 and 14:1) and placed on the forehead of those who worship the beast. It is also on the forehead of the prostitute of Babylon, representing the spiritual adultery of pagans who worship false gods (Revelation 17:5).

Verse 4

We will see in a moment that the saved are only Jews. It does not mention Christians at all. However, this explanation begins with the reassurance that Christians will be among the saved. We see the number 144,000. Let's first look at the 144. That is the sum of 12 x 12. The twelve tribal patriarchs of Israel represent the saved of the Old Testament. The twelve apostles represent the saved of the New Testament. Thus twelve times itself is 144. (See the numbers chart.)

What about the thousand? Once again, refer to the numbers

chart. Ten represents all-inclusiveness. One thousand is the sum total of 10 X 10 X 10. In other words, the all-inclusive saved times the all-inclusive saved times the all-inclusive saved. This is intense. This is reassurance. No one among the saved is going to be left out or forgotten or disqualified. All the saved times all the saved times all the saved will be saved!

Verses 5-8

Since the history is being told all over again, we are back in the era covered by the Old Testament.

Judah is listed as the oldest of Israel's (Jacob's) sons. But was he? His first three were disinherited as head of the family for the following reasons:

Reuben married his step-mother, Bilhah, the mother of his step-brothers, Dan and Naphtali. In that era, it was a way of declaring a son was now head of the family, head of the tribe. (See Genesis 30:3, 8; 35:22-23; 49:3-4.)

Simeon killed all the males in the town of a Canaanite who had violated his sister, Dinah. He took all their wealth, their women, and their children. It put fear in his father, Israel, that the rest of the Canaanites would retaliate, attack, and obliterate his own tribe. (See Genesis 34:1-2, 25-29; 35:23; 49:5-7.)

Levi helped his brother, Simeon, kill all those Canaanites. (See Genesis 34:1-2, 25-29; 35:23; 49:5-7.)

Therefore, father Israel/Jacob gave the scepter (of being head of the family, and inheritor of all Israel had) to Judah (Genesis 49:9-10).

Gad is listed next to Reuben, the firstborn of all the sons, and was the firstborn of Leah by her handmade, Zilpah (Genesis 35:26). Asher was the second born of Leah's handmaid (Genesis 35:26). Naphtali was the second born of Rachel's handmaid, Bilhah.

[Dan is left out of this list in Revelation. He was the firstborn of Rachel's handmaid and Israel's fifth son (Genesis 35:25). Israel called Dan a serpent (Genesis 49:16-17). Satan is referred to as being a serpent (Genesis 3:1 and II Corinthians 11:3). When King Jeroboam made two golden calves for the Israelites to worship, he placed one of them in the territory of Dan (I Kings 12:28-29). In his place is Manasseh.]

Manasseh, Joseph's son, was claimed by Israel/Jacob as his own. Though a second-born (like Jacob was who usurped his older brother, Esau ~ Genesis 27). Manasseh was considered by Jacob as Joseph's firstborn (Genesis 48:17-19).

Simeon is Israel's and Leah's second-born son (Genesis 35:23).

Levi is Israel's third-born son and Judah his fourth son by Leah (Genesis 35:23).

Issachar is Israel's fifth-born son by Leah (Genesis 35:24).

Zebulun is Israel's sixth-born son by Leah (Genesis 35:24).

Joseph is listed a second time (actually, it was his son who was listed before him), but this time as Rachel's firstborn (Genesis 35:24-25).

Benjamin is listed as Israel's second-born son by Rachel (Genesis 35:24).

Of each of the twelve tribes, each had 12,000 who were saved. If we take this literally, then the same number of people were saved from each tribe (not likely!), and all had to be Jews. But taken figuratively, using the table of numbers, all of the saved in each tribe were saved and none left out.

Verse 9

Then comes the reassurance that all people in Old Testament times, not just Jews, could be saved. There were godly people in all nations and of all languages. Think about Job. Genesis 36 lists the descendants of Esau, the brother of Israel/Jacob, who became known as the Edomites. Verse 33 lists Jobab as a king of the Edomites. It fits Job in the Bible. Even though the Edomites worshiped idols, Job did not. He worshiped the true God.

Think about Nebuchadnezzar and Darius, and Cyrus in the book of Daniel who at different times believed in the true God. Think about Jonah who went to Nineveh in Assyria, warned the king to tell his people to behave, and the king led his subjects in repentance before the true God (Jonah 3:1-10), and Nahum who later prophesied to them. Consider the prophet Obadiah who prophesied to the people of Edom. The major prophets also prophesied at different times to Egypt, Babylon, Tyre, etc. Later, look at the magi (wise men) who went to see Jesus as a child in Bethlehem (Matthew 2:21-12). Even in Romans 1 and 2, Paul explains non-Jews who believed out of instinct due to evidences of nature, and a God-given conscience, and concluded that none of them was without a valid excuse (verses 19-22).

So now God shows that even the righteous non-Jews are saved, and able to wear white robes of purity.

What is the significance of the palm branches? According to Josephus, they were placed as a canopy over the altar in the temple on the first day of the Feast of Trumpets (Leviticus 23:4), the Day of Atonement (Leviticus 23:27), the fifteenth day of the Feast of Tabernacles and for that whole week (Leviticus 2:34-40), and the first and fifteenth day of the Feast of Passover (Leviticus 23:4-8).

Verses 10-12

Then the cheers begin, for the innumerable crowd cries out as with one voice, *Salvation belongs to our God!* Yes, salvation was not just available to the Jews in Old Testament times, but to non-Jews who did the best they could without the Law of Moses to love and honor the one true God. *Who sits on the throne!* Yes, God is the king of our hearts, our lives, our very being. Though not Jews, they have their own special love for God. *And to the Lamb!* Indeed, Jesus died for everyone. Paul says all with faith have always been children of Abraham (Galatians 3:7-9) who lived before the Jewish nation existed. The saving power of Jesus' death on the cross was retroactive to those who lived under the Law (Romans 3:25; Hebrews 9:15 and 10:12)

And now the innumerable crowd multiplies again. The angels, who once again are greatly influenced to worship God by the example of humans, join in the drama. Now the angels bow down on their faces before the throne and worship. They cannot shout on their faces. But they can utter the quiet Amen. Then they whisper from deep in their being, *Praise....Glory....Wisdom....Thanks....Honor....Power....Strength....* Whose? *Be to our God.* Yes, he is the God of humans who are saved, and of angels. *Forever. And Ever.* Then they utter once again their quiet *Amen.*

Verses 13-74

But there is more information, now, about those non-Jews with their white robes. One of the elders ~ perhaps Judah, perhaps Joseph, who knows? ~ asks John who they are and where they came from. It is a rhetorical question.

The elder says they are not just ordinary people who were saved. They are people who were persecuted during their lifetime. Can you imagine people living in pagan families, cities, and nations? Can you imagine the number of families who disowned the convert? The number of neighborhoods where they had to endure insults and perhaps beatings in dark alleys? The number of cities where they lost their job and maybe even their home? The number of nations where they were imprisoned and tortured and killed?

Think about Job whose friends thought they had God all figured out and blamed Job for his own tragedies ~ the rustling of his herds, the killing of his children, and the monstrous disease he was enduring ~ in the idolatrous land Moab. Think about Shadrach, Meshach and Abednego who were thrown into a furnace for refusing to bow down to an idol during the time of King Nebuchadnezzar (Daniel 3). Think about Daniel who was thrown into a lair of lions for refusing to give up praying to the only true God during the time of Darius (Daniel 6). Of course, the same thing happened in the Christian era among converts who left paganism.

Yes, even though not many of their stories are told in the Bible, non-Jewish martyrs did exist, they did endure, and they were saved. And now they are ever before the throne of God serving him day and night. Now no more losing jobs and going hungry. Now no more running for their lives with not even water to drink as the sun beats mercilessly on them in their wanderings.

Now the Lamb on the throne is their shepherd, and God has wiped away their tears.

Chapter 8. Seven Trumpets of Historic Reminders ~ God Punishes the Punishers

Verse 1

After rejoicing by the Jews who were saved, and the non-Jews who were saved, as though pondering all the amazing events, something strange happens. "Silence."

The Greek word here is *sige* referring to a silence that is commanded. Not just any silence, but silence as in the calm before the storm. We've had a lot of celebrating. Things are about to change.

Sigao means to keep silence or keep something concealed. Romans 16:25 refers to the mystery hidden for long ages past, and I Peter 1:12 refers to the prophets who wrote of salvation, but the angels didn't even understand it.

Hour in the Bible before clocks refers to a span of time, all the time, or a season. In John 2:4, Jesus said his hour had not yet come. Paul said in I Corinthians 15:30 "We endanger ourselves every hour".

Look at the chart on numbers. Half refers to being in the middle of something or part of something. For part of the time, God's prophets prophesied to those who were not living right and were persecuting his true followers. Oh, how God wants everyone to repent and come to safety. He sends prophet after prophet to warn them of the danger their actions are taking them into.

God is patient with us, for he does not want anyone to perish, (II Peter 3:9) but his patience with persecutors lasts only so long (Deuteronomy 32:35; Romans 12:19). Now it is the silence before something important happens

Verses 2-5

Seven angels are given seven trumpets. Remember seven represents heaven (3) and earth (4). (See the numbers chart.) Something is about to happen that will involve both heaven and earth.

But, during the silence something else important is done. Incense is offered to God.

Incense was offered every day in the Holy Place of the temple in Jerusalem. The altar of incense was just a few feet away from the curtain that hid the Holy of Holies with God's Presence above the ark of the covenant. Offering incense was a special honor given to only some of the priests (Luke 1:8-10).

What is the incense being offered in heaven? Remember, everything in Revelation is symbolic. The incense represents the prayers of the saints. How important our prayers are. Daniel 9 explains how our prayers can affect the work of God's angels as they fight Satan's angels. We must pray without ceasing. Pray for our family members, our next-door neighbors, members of our congregation, our schools, our city, our nation, our world.

Pray in silence. Don't always be shouting and singing. Stop. Listen for the silence. Then pray. Pray short prayers. Pray long prayers. Pray aloud. Pray in your mind. But pray. Pray without ceasing (I Thessalonians 5:17). Prayer is the most powerful thing on this earth, along with the Word of God. Remember, God loves to answer prayer. And in this story, he is about to do just that.

Then the angel does something strange. Once he burns the incense that had been in his censer, he fills it again; only this time it is with the fire on the incense altar. Jeremiah 15:14 refers to the fire kindled in God's anger, and Isaiah 66:15 refers to being rebuked with flames of fire. The angel hurls the fire onto the earth. Then come the thunder, rumblings, flashes of lightning and earthquake.

The silence is broken.

Verses 6-9

Trumpets were used to call multitudes to attention to special events. They were used in the temple to call Jews to attend the special annual feasts of rejoicing, and in wartime to call men to battle (Numbers 10:9-10). Both are about to occur, for God is going to take vengeance on those who mistreated his people, and the people will rejoice.

What we have here in the trumpets is a retelling of major parts of the history of the Jews. God first used the enemies of God's people to chastise them when they sometimes went astray, like a loving father does his children (Hebrews 12:6). But then God punishes the punishers.

Trumpet 1

Hail and fire mixed with blood are hurled down on earth and part of the vegetation/crops are destroyed.

Egypt punished the Israelites and made them their slaves. Therefore, in Exodus 7:17, God through Moses turned the Nile River to blood. Exodus 9:23-24 says God through Moses sent thunder, hail, lightning, and fire mixed with the hail down onto the Egyptians, trying to convince them that the God of Moses is the true God, and to let his people go.

Trumpet 2

A mountain plunges into the sea, one-third of living creatures and ships with their crew and passengers die, and one-third of the sea turns to blood.

Tyre took advantage of the people of Jerusalem when they were under siege. They never tried to help them. When the city was finally taken by the Babylonians and completely burned and leveled, the people of Tyre rejoiced (Ezekiel 26:2). Because of this, the seafarers of Tyre perished (Ezekiel 26:17-18).

Verses 10-11

Trumpet 3

A great star crashes to the earth into rivers and springs. The star is named Wormwood and turns the waters bitter. Wormwood refers to undrinkable water, gall, poison. Jeremiah 9:15 refers to bitter food and poisonous water. Deuteronomy 29:18 refers to idolatry as a drink of bitter poison.

The idolatrous Babylonians enslaved the southern tribes of Israel. Isaiah 14:3 tells of God giving relief to the southern tribes of Israelites after their bondage in Babylon. In verses 12-15, Isaiah refers to the so-called "morning star" falling from heaven for wanting to be above God with his own throne. The true morning is Jesus (Revelation 22:16). Daniel 3 tells of a great image Nebuchadnezzar made for everyone to bow down to. Was it an image of himself? He later referred to the immense empire he had built "for the glory of my majesty" (Daniel 4:30).

The Assyrians enslave the northern tribes of Israel. In Nahum 1:8 and 2:5-6, God destroys Nineveh, capital of the Assyrians who took the northern tribes of Israel into bondage. How? With an overwhelming flood. Wormwood

Verse 12

Trumpet 4

The sun, moon and stars are darkened, affecting part of the earth.

Egypt was punished at another time for taking advantage of Israel during war (Ezekiel 29:2; 32:7).

Babylon was punished for worshiping their king (Isaiah 13:1, 10).

Tyre and Sidon were punished for selling Israelites to the Greeks as their slaves (Joel 3:4-6; 15).

Verse 13

There are now going to be three woes. These three woes will accompany the last three trumpets ~ five, six, and seven. These woes will bring dreaded sorrow on God's people's enemies. Yes, God's children may suffer for awhile. But God knows what is going on. He warns their abusers.

Yes, God is noticing. God noticed then. God notices still today. He notices when someone loses a job for being a Christian, just like he did back then. He notices when someone's family disowns the convert for becoming a Christian, just like he did back then. He notices when someone is fined for trumped-up charges, just like he did back then. He notices the taunts, the secret beatings, the stealing of self-respect meted out by God's enemies onto Christians, just like he did back then.

It may seem as though God doesn't care. But he does care. The job of each person who is persecuted is to not blame God. That is what Satan wants because he thinks he has convinced people he doesn't exist. Each time we endure abuse, Satan loses and God wins. Each time we refuse to turn away from our Christianity in the face of more threats, Satan loses and God wins. Each time we survive the unendurable meted out by God's enemies onto his children, Satan loses and God wins. And even if we don't survive, Satan still loses, God still wins, and you arise triumphant in the heavenly throne room.

Chapter 9. Seven Trumpets of Historic Reminders ~ Israelites Chastised

TRUMPET FIVE

WOE ONE

Remember, Revelation is a love letter. In parts of his letter, God reminds us that he always did whatever was necessary to keep his children close to him so he could protect us. But sometimes in the past they left him, like a wayward child. So, he had to go get them, chastise them, and hold them close again. Then, always, after punishing them so they would do right again, he would punish his punishers.

Each time we are given this reminder, it is a reminder that, when we are going through our own hardships, perhaps God is chastising a nation so they will come back to him. Families and neighbors and governments can be cruel. It shows them for what they are when we suffer under them. But always, we are reassured that they won't get by with treating us like dung. God says he will take vengeance on our enemies (Romans 12:19), and eventually he always does. What reassurance Revelation is when life is hard for us because we chose to be Christians, to follow Jesus Christ as the Son of God.

Verse 1

The star falls from heaven. Not a star, but the star. The same fake "morning star" is mentioned in Trumpet Three. The star is explained in Isaiah 14:4, 12-14 as the one who fell from heaven because he wanted to be God. Although Luke 10:18 calls him Lucifer, in Isaiah, he is incarnate in the king of Babylon.

He is given a key. What is the significance of a key? Isaiah

22:22 refers to the key to the house of David, the Kingdom of Israel. In Mathew 16:18-19 and 18:1,18, Jesus gives the keys of the new kingdom, the church, to the apostles (not just Peter). In Revelation 3:7, Jesus has the key of David which is explained in Romans 1:3-4 as the eternal kingdom, the church. In Revelation 3:7, Jesus has the key of David which is explained in Romans 1:3-4 as the eternal kingdom, the church. In Revelation 1:18 Jesus has the keys of Hades (the grave) and Death.

Lucifer incarnate in the king of Babylon, is given the key to the bottomless pit, the abyss. It comes from the Greek word *phrear*, meaning a well or a deep dungeon. This is not hell. It is Satan's home, Satan's kingdom.

Verses 2-4

The abyss is like a gigantic furnace, similar to hell as explained by Jesus in Matthew 13:42, 49-50. Out of this bottomless pit comes locusts. Joel says in 1:2-15 that they are there to chastise Israel for worshiping false gods and being immoral. But they are more lethal than locusts, for they have the power of scorpions.

Scorpions have venom that is used to either kill their prey, or paralyze them so they can be eaten. It is fast acting, allowing the scorpion to easily capture their prey. Severe reactions and death from stings are common among humans, and cause thousands of deaths a year worldwide, ten times more than from snake bites.

These locusts are told not to attack greenery as locusts normally do. Instead, they are to harm people, but not kill them. Why? We know from the context of the entire Old Testament, that God had to sometimes chastise his people in order to bring them back to him. He loves his people, and he does not enjoy chastising them, but he will for their sake. Oh, how he misses his children when we do wrong.

Specifically, which Jews were to be harmed? God's people, who had fallen away from him and no longer had the seal of God on their foreheads. Remember, the seal of God is the seal of salvation.

Back to Joel, after the Israelites are chastised, 3:2 says he will eventually punish Israel's punishers.

Verses 5-6

Remember, the stinging locusts were not to kill them, but only hurt them. Most species of scorpions are incapable of delivering enough venom to kill a human, although they can kill the very young or old or already-sick. The effects of the scorpion sting include vomiting, cramps, blurred vision, sensitivity to light, hyper salivation, difficulty swallowing, and agitation. Since the Israelites are chastised by being taken to Babylon as captives, they indeed would experience agitation ~ a lot of it.

How long does the chastisement last? Five months. Look at the chart on numbers. Five is half of all-inclusiveness. Months is referred to by Job in 14:5 and 21:21 as a lifetime. So five simply means half of a lifetime. The Israelites were captives in Babylon for seventy years, though it was the royal family who went first, then later more important people, and finally middle-class people. So some were not in Babylon the entire seventy years. Some of the Jews who were forced to leave Jerusalem were later freed and went back to Jerusalem where they lamented things weren't as they used to be (Ezra 3:12).

Verses 7-10

These attackers have the shape of locusts. Locusts have a swarming instinct, and armies of them can invade and completely devastate a land. But they also have the shape of battle horses.

Joel 2:4 says basically the same thing about the invading locusts that destroy everything in their path: "They have the appearance of horses; they gallop along like cavalry".

They have gold crowns and teeth like lions. Joel 1:6 refers to the locusts as an invading nation whose power is without number, with teeth of a lion. They also have human faces. Remember, we are talking symbolism; Revelation must be read as symbolism to be understood. In Joel 3:1, he explains that the locusts are powerful nations come to scatter God's people around the world and divide up their land as their chastisement.

Having hair like a woman refers to God's accusing his bride of adultery. Hosea 4:10-13 explains that idolatry is adultery. Indeed, the Jews had forsaken the one true God and gone running after false gods.

The locusts have breastplates of iron, and their wings sound like war chariots, all descriptions of warriors.

In summary, we are reminded that they have tails like scorpions where the venomous stinger is, but they are only to hurt ~ not kill, but hurt ~ for five months, half a lifetime.

Verses 11-12

These invading "locusts" sent to chastise the Israelites have a king. Their king is the angel of the bottomless pit and named Abaddon in Hebrew and Apollyon in Greek. Both words mean destroyer.

There are two woes in Revelation. The first one is trumpet 5 where God's people are chastised so they will return to him. Woe one is now past. Now is the time to punish the punisher.

TRUMPET 6

WOE TWO

Verses 13-14

Now the sixth trumpet of historic reminders is blasted, and a single voice comes from the four horns on the throne. There were four horns on the altars of incense and sacrifices (Exodus 27:2; 30:1-2). Psalm 18:2 and Luke 1:69 refer to God as the horn of our salvation. Four horns of salvation, then, would refer to salvation for people on earth, four being the number that represents the earth (see numbers chart).

God calls out that the Euphrates River is no longer to be held back. The Euphrates River is the river of Babylon (today's Iraq). Jeremiah 51:60-64 describes Babylon this way. Idolatrous Babylon is the kingdom that held captive the Israelites seventy years to chastise them and bring them back to God, though they didn't know that's why they were doing it.

Verses 15-16

Now the angels are released to punish the punishers.

Hour represents the beginning of a special time (John 2:4) Day represents the beginning of a special time (Zechariah 14:8-9). Month represents a lifetime (John 14:5; 21:21). Year represents the beginning of a special time (Isaiah 61:1-2). So, we are about to learn of a special event during the lifetime (prime of life?) of God's enemies, the Babylonians. Since one-fourth refers to "part of", we can assume one-third also means a part of.

There are two hundred million mounted troops. Two in Jewish number symbolism represents strength. (See the numbers chart.) Ten represents all-inclusiveness, so a million would be all armies times all armies infinitely, as though all the armies of the world were going after Babylon to conquer it. Daniel 5 is about the son of Nebuchadnezzar, the conqueror of the Israelites. During the son's reign, Darius the Great of Persia conquered Babylon. The Persian Empire was the largest empire in world history at the time. It spanned all the Middle East, much of Asia, must of Africa, and much of Europe

Verses 17-19

The horsemen wear breastplates of fiery red, dark, hyacinth blue, and sulfur yellow. Sometimes red represents blood, but in this case it represents fire. The blue is a smoky, dark blue, representing smoke. The sulfur yellow represents brimstone.

Out of the horses' mouths come fire, smoke, and brimstone. In the Old Testament, brimstone represents pitch or tar that smells when it burns. In the New Testament, brimstone represents sulfur, also which smells when it burns. Their tails are snakes with fangs, able to poison that which survives the horses' heads.

The red, blue, and yellow are further identified as plagues which killed a portion of mankind. In this case, it is the Babylonians. The Persian Empire had around 150,000 troops, plus the troops of their allies. The population of the city of Babylon was approximately 500,000 at that time. So, if all troops were used to attack Babylon, there would be approximately one soldier for every three people.

Verses 20-21

Even though God punished the enemies of his people, he did not punish them all. Would the rest of the world take notice how God protects his people? Apparently they do not. For the rest of the world continued then and continues still today to indulge in the idolatry of fame, fortune, beauty, and power. They murder the innocent to maintain what they possess and obtain even more.

They lure people with promises of making them famous and rich and beautiful and powerful, but they lie just as Satan lied to Adam and Eve in the Garden of Eden, promising they would become as smart as God by following him. Instead, Satan stole their freedom from them. The famous, rich, beautiful and powerful still steal from the people. Interestingly, even the unfamous, unrich, unbeautiful, and unpowerful often commit sexual immoralities, claiming what is between two consenting adults, is acceptable to God ~ another lie.

The battle against sin to protect God's people is never-ending. Everyone keeps sinning. Everyone is a sinner. No one can get it right, no matter how hard we try. Look at Romans 7 to see the scope and depth of this problem with mankind. How God's heart breaks when he sees it.

Some day there must be a Day of Judgment. But God does not want anyone to perish (II Peter 3:9). Yes, God punishes the incorrigible who hurt his children. But what about everyone else? Are they sinning out of ignorance? Do they want to do right, but can't seem to make themselves do it all? What to do about the ordinary sinner?

The seventh trumpet is not allowed yet to sound, for the event is the Day of Judgment.

Chapter 10. Seven Thunders of Judgment; Day of Judgment Postponed

Verse 1

John's vision has apparently taken him to earth. Now a mighty angel comes out of heaven to him. He is clothed in a cloud. The angel's face is like the sun, and his feet like pillars of fire

There is a rainbow around his head. Following is a description of a mighty angel described in Daniel 10:6 who fought side by side with Michael, the Archangel: "His body was like chrysotile, his face like lightning, his eyes like flaming torches, his arms and legs like the gleam of burnished bronze, and his voice like the sound of a multitude."

Verses 2-4

The angel covers both land and sea, and has in his hand a little book. No seals on this book. It is open.

The angel roars like a lion. Then seven thunders charge through the sky and speak something. Thunder represents God's power (Job 26:14). Thunders also represent punishment through earthquake, storm, and flame of fire. These seven thunders are the thunders of judgment and punishment.

John, who is writing in his own book of all he is seeing is interrupted and says he cannot tell anyone what the seven thunders of judgment just said.

Indeed, God could have held court centuries ago. He could do it now. But he does not. Why? Because all have sinned and come short of the glory of God (Romans 3:23), and the wages we earn when we sin is death ~ physical death and spiritual death. God loves us. He is not ready or willing to condemn the world. Something must be done.

Someone must pay those wages. There are certain natural spiritual laws. For example, it is impossible for God to lie (Hebrews 6:18). It is impossible for Satan to tell the truth (John 8:44). God is truth and his very words are truth (John 14:17; 17:17). Therefore, if

God lied, he would go out of existence. Another spiritual law is that the moment we sin, our soul dies, and later our body dies. God said so in the Garden of Eden (Genesis 2:17). The penalty, the fine, the wage must be paid. It is a spiritual law.

God has been planning for the result of sin to be paid. For centuries he planned and predicted it. Man is too weak to pay the wages and survive. God must send someone to do it for us.

Verses 5-7

The angel with the little book raises his right hand toward heaven, and swears by him who created the heavens and the earth. Who did create them? Genesis 1:1-2 say God and his Holy Spirit created them. John 1:1-2 says Jesus, the Word, created them.

Then the angel declares, "There will be no more delay." In the Greek, "time" is *chronos,* meaning a long time, awhile, a season, a time period. The seventh trumpet of history must now be blown. As soon as the mystery of God is accomplished, as prophesied, the seventh trumpet can sound.

Verse 8

What is the mystery? Here are all the scriptures in the New Testament that include the word "mystery".

Matthew 13:1-10, 34-35 *says the mystery is the kingdom of heaven, known since the foundation of the world.*
Romans 10:1; 11:1-12, 19, 25-17, 35 *explains that it is complete forgiveness of sins.*
Romans 16:24-27 *says it is the grace of the Lord Jesus Christ, known since the world began.*
I Corinthians 1:2, 17; 2:7-9 *says it is the cross of Christ, known about since before the world began.*
I Corinthians 1:2; 3:19 – 4:5 *says all, including Christ, belong to Christians.*
I Corinthians 15:50-57 *says it is Christians raising from death to immortality.*

Ephesians 1:1-4, 9-10 *says it will be Christians being without blame, known since before the foundation of the world.*
Ephesians 3:3-4, 9 *says it is Christians who have access to the riches of Christ, and has been known from the beginning of the world.*
Ephesians 5:30-32 *says it is Christians who are one with Christ.*
Colossians 1:23-28 *says it is Christ, the hope of glory, who is in Christians, and has been known before all ages and generations.*
Colossians 1:1; 2:2-3 *says it is Christians who have risen with Christ.*
Colossians 3:24; 4:3-6 *says it is Christians receiving the reward of Christ.*
II Thessalonians 2:2, 10 *says it is that the wicked will be destroyed.*
I Timothy 3:15-16 *says it is the resurrection of Jesus.*
Revelation 17:7-9, 14, 17 *says it is the Lamb overcoming the beast, known from the foundation of the world.*

It is obvious to us what the mystery is: It is salvation, being saved from spiritual death and hell through the blood of Jesus Christ. It has been delayed, but all is ready now. People of the world have had thousands of years to get it right, to be sinless. Some were guided by the Law of Moses which, if kept exactly, would make the observer perfect. But no one was ever able to. Some were guided by instinct and conscience, but that didn't make mankind perfect either. All are doomed because "All have sinned and come short of the glory of God" (Romans 3:23), and the wages of sin is death (Romans 6:23).

The prophets have predicted it for long enough. The seventh trumpet of history cannot sound until the event has taken place. Now is the time for that event.

Verses 9-11

The mighty angel with the little book with the part of the history that yet needs to be played out, gives it to John. John is told to eat the words. To drink in the words. To absorb the words.

It is sweet in his mouth. The law of the Lord converts the soul (Psalm 19:7-11). The words of God are pleasant and sweet to the soul (Proverbs 16:24). The wisdom of God ever gives hope

(Proverbs 24:13-14).

While Jesus was with us on earth, he spoke amazing words and performed astounding miracles. He was so popular, the politicians were jealous of him. He was so popular, the people were ready to make him their king. They even publicly declared him king when he entered Jerusalem (Matthew 21:1-11). How sweet everything was. How wonderful everything was.

But it turns bitter in John's stomach. Something is terribly wrong. What is it?

The mighty angel tells John he is about to write the prophecy of world nations and languages. Once done, the seventh trumpet can sound.

Chapter 11. Predictions and Preview of the Life of Christ

WOE TWO

Verse 1

John is told to measure the temple and the altar. Ezekiel had measured the temple and everything around it (Ezekiel 40:5; 42:15), but the dimensions of the earthly temple are too limiting. Everyone in the world cannot fit into it. There must be a spiritual temple. But how do you measure a spiritual temple? You measure its value. I Corinthians 3:16 says Christians are the temple of God; so, instead of going to the temple, the temple comes to us. Hebrews 11:23-twenty-four says Jesus would enter the Most Holy Place of the tabernacle (temple) not made with hands, which is in heaven.

John is also told to count the worshipers there. How do you measure people? You measure their lives.

One man was weighed and found wanting (Daniel 5:1, 4, 27). Jesus measured the Jews' forefathers who murdered the prophets (Matthew 23:31-32). Paul referred to the measure of faith (Romans 12:3) and the measure of our Christian life (II Corinthians 10:12-13).

Verse 2

But John is told not to measure the Gentiles, because they are going to trample the holy city forty-two months. Forty-two months is 1260 days, which is three and a half years.

Read Daniel 2:36-43 about coming world powers. Verses 36-38 refer to Babylonian empire. Verse 39 (also Daniel 11:2) refers the empires of Persia and Greece. Verse 40 (also Daniel 11:3) refers to the Roman Empire.

More specifically, Daniel predicted in 2:44 the trampling would be during the time of the fourth kingdom that God's kingdom would appear and never be destroyed. Colossians 1:13 and 18 refer to the kingdom as being the church. Indeed, the Gentiles trampled the holy city with its Gentile Governor Pilate and his soldiers ever ready to make sure the people cower to Rome's laws and wishes.

Daniel 7:23, 25, 27 says the fourth kingdom, will persecute the saints for a time, times, and half a time.

Time equals one year. Times equals two years. Half a time equals half a year. So the Gentiles will persecute the saints three and a half years, the time that Jesus preached under the jurisdiction of the Roman government.

Verses 3-4

But while this is going on, two of God's witnesses will prophecy 1260 days. When we multiply 42 months by 30 days, we get 1260 days. This is the same length of time Jesus preached and performed miracles, and it is during this time that Gentiles controlled Israel.

The two witnesses are also called two olive trees and two lampstands. And why two? When we look at the numbers chart, we see that two represents strength, power.

In the tabernacle standing in the Holy Place near the entrance to the Most Holy Place was a lampstand. It was to have six branches on one side holding six small lamps*-, and six branches on the other side holding six small lamps (Exodus 25:31-32). The oil for the lamps was to be made from olives of an olive tree. They were to be kept burning all day (Exodus 27:20-21).

Psalms 119:105 says God's Word is a lamp unto our feet. John 14:17 and 17:17 says God's Word is truth and is the Comforter from God.

The two witnesses were to prophesy. The word prophecy in Greek means to pour out. What were they to pour out? The word of God.

This is to be the job of the two witnesses, but just what or who will they be? There are two witnesses to Jesus' baptism: The Holy Spirit descended on him like a dove, and the Father spoke out of heaven (Luke 3:21-22 and 4:14, 40-41). Later Jesus said his testimony was not valid if he testified of himself. He had [1] the Father who testified concerning him in the prophecies (John 5:36-40), and [2] his miracles (John 10:25).

Verses 5-6

Remember, two is symbolic for strength (see the numbers chart). The two witnesses are to have power over the heavens and the earth. When Jesus was on earth, he controlled the heavens when he calmed two storms ~ one with just three words, "Peace! Be still!" (Mark 4:35-41), and one just by putting his foot into a boat (Mark 6:45-52). On earth, he made a hand full of loaves and fishes feed thousands (Mark 6:30-44).

As his enemies were going to try to stop the two witnesses, fire will come out of their mouth. The Lord told Jeremiah that, he was making the words in Jeremiah's mouth to be fire (Jeremiah 5:14). In Isaiah 66:16 God said with fire and a sword he would judge the world. What comes out of Jesus' mouth? A sword (Revelation 1:16). I Corinthians 3:13 says we are tried by fire, and I Peter 1:7 says our faith is refined by fire. Therefore, we see the fire coming out of the witnesses' mouth is the judgmental words of God.

Verses 7-11

Next the beast is to come up from the bottomless pit. This is not hell; it is Satan's home, Satan's realm. The beast, Satan, is predicted to kill the two witnesses ~ Jesus with his prophecies and miracles. The next statement comes right out and says what Sodom and Egypt are ~ the place where Jesus is to be crucified.

For three and a half days, people of all nations will refuse to bury them. They will not able to bury and hide the miracles Jesus performed, because he will perform them on too many people who will tell about it. They will not be able to bury and hide the prophecies of Jesus that had been around for centuries, and their fulfillment will not be denied.

During that time people will gloat over having killed the two witnesses ~ Jesus' miracles and prophecies fulfilled.

But then the great miracle. After three and one-half days, breath will return to the two witnesses. This three and one-half can refer to the amount of time Jesus preached and performed miracles to prove he really was the Son of God, come to save the world. It can also refer to the three days Jesus was in the grave (Matthew 12:40), but it is more probable it is referring to the years of his ministry. Regardless, Jesus' enemies are terrified.

Verses 12-14

Finally, it is foretold to John that the two witnesses then will ascend to heaven amidst an earthquake. When Jesus dies there will be an earthquake (Matthew 27:54). When Jesus comes back to life, there will be an earthquake (Matthew 28:2). Isaiah 13:11-13 refers to God's anger at the arrogant sinful as an earthquake.

Then one-tenth of the city will fall. Since ten refers to all-inclusiveness, one-tenth would refer to just a few. Why would only one-tenth of the city fall? God planned to give people a chance to repent (II Peter 3:9).

After that, 7,000 people will be killed. Remember, seven means everywhere, including heaven (3) and earth (4). Of course, ten refers to all-inclusiveness; so thousand would be 10 X 10 X 10. (See the chart on numbers.) Therefore, everyone doomed to die spiritually, will do just that.

However, eventually, everyone on earth will fear and glorify God, bowing to Jesus Christ and confessing him as Lord (Romans 14:11-12).

This is the end of the second woe. It is the destiny of those who reject Jesus. The third woe will occur in Revelation 12.

TRUMPET SEVEN

Verses 15-16

Now that we have had a preview of the final events, the events where the good-hearted people who at least try, can be saved, we preview the last trumpet call.

At the last trumpet, Jesus will descend in the clouds (I Thessalonians 4:16-17), and we will ascend to meet him. And we shall ever be with him. Now Jesus can deliver the kingdom, the church, to God (I Corinthians 15:24).

At last the grand announcement.

The kingdom of this world. Yes, Satan's kingdom. Jesus has snatched it out of his hand. Now, at last, it *has become the kingdom of our Lord and of his Christ!* The battle is over! The battle has been won! Good has triumphed over evil! At last! At last.... *And he will reign forever and ever!* Oh, yes, Lord Jesus. You, our commander, our general, who paid the wage of death to Satan for us, to you belongs all honor. We worship you!

Verse 17-18

Now, back in heaven, the twenty-four elders leave their thrones, and fall on their faces. The twenty-four who represent all the saved of the Old Testament era (through the 12 Tribes of Israel) plus all the saved of the New Testament era (through the 12 apostles).

Once again, this is a quiet time because one cannot shout while bowing down onto one's face. And so they whisper their prayer.

We give thanks to you, Lord God Almighty, comes the deep sigh. Yes, we give thanks now and will keep giving thanks from now on without end because we can never thank you enough. *The One who is and who was.* Yes, you are the eternal one, and all this time, you never forgot us. *You have taken your great power and have begun to reign.* You are all-deserving. We humans tried, but never could. It took a part of God to come to earth as one of us to rescue us. Oh, God, the plan. So amazing. So loving. So holy.

Then will come the time when all those people who punished God's loved ones ~ whether with mockery or murder ~ with no remorse will be punished. *The nations were angry, and your wrath has come.* We wondered sometimes if you noticed how they laughed at us and derided us and tortured us and killed us. You did notice, Lord God. You did notice.

The time has come for judging the [spiritually] dead, and for rewarding your servants the prophets. Sometimes the prophets didn't even understand what they were writing about, but now they do, now that Jesus has come and conquered. *And your saints and those who reverence your name, both small and great.* We do revere you, Lord God. On our faces we give up our pride, our ego, our being, all for you. Only you are worthy. *And for destroying those who destroy the earth.* Peace, at last. With no more enemies. Just peace. Holy peace. Reverent peace. Safe in the arms of Jesus.

Verse 19

Then, at last, the temple in heaven will be opened. On earth, only priests were allowed into the temple itself, made up of the Holy Place and the Most Holy Place. Finally, it will be opened for everyone, for all the saved are God's priests (Revelation 1:6).

Then, too, the Ark of the Covenant will be seen. It had never been available for anyone to see, including other priests. Only the high priest could go into the to see the Ark of the Covenant, and only then just once a year on the Day of Atonement. (See Leviticus 16:2-17.)

Jesus will become the curtain hiding the Most Holy Place (Hebrews 10:20), and after his body is torn on the cross, the curtain will be torn too (Matthew 27:51).

God's people will no longer kept from the temple. Now, we will be able to serve him day and night in his temple in heaven (Revelation 7:15).

Now the preview is over. What follows in future chapters is a detailed retelling of Jesus' birth, life, death, and triumphant resurrection.

Chapter 12. Jesus' Birth & The Birth of Christianity….

Verse 1

Who is the woman clothed with the sun with the moon under her feet and a crown of twelve stars?

Ezekiel 16:1-14 speaks of God's love affair with Israel, starting with their infancy until he made them his bride. In verse 8 he says, "I gave you my solemn oath and entered into a covenant with you, declares the Sovereign Lord, and you became mine."

In Hosea 2:19, God says he has betrothed Israel to him forever. And in Isaiah 54:5-6, he said, "Your Maker is your husband."

This woman has a crown of 12 stars. Of course this represents the Twelve Tribes of Israel.

Verse 2

She is pregnant, in pain and about to give birth. Who is she giving birth to? As already seen in the preview, Jesus is to be born and begin preaching during the time of the Roman Empire. Daniel predicted this in 7:21-23, the Roman Empire being fourth after the Grecian, Persian, and Babylonian empires. But Daniel gets much more specific than this.

Daniel 9:24: "Seventy-sevens are decreed for your people and your holy city to finish transgression, to put an end to sin, to atone for wickedness, to bring in everlasting righteousness, to seal up vision and prophecy, and to anoint the most holy." Seventy times seven is 490 years.

Daniel 9:25: "Know and understand this: From the issuing of the decree to restore and rebuild Jerusalem until the Anointed One, the ruler, comes, there will be seven sevens, and sixty-two sevens." Seven sevens is 49. Sixty-two sevens if 434. Add the two together, and you get 483 years.

Daniel 9:27: "He will confirm a covenant with many for one seven. In the middle of the seven, he will put an end to sacrifice and offering." The middle of 7 is 3-1/2.

In 520 BC, King Darius sent Ezra to Jerusalem to start rebuilding it, starting with the temple. Thirty years after 520 BC is 490 BC. Ezra states that building the temple was interrupted in the second year of King Darius of Persia because their enemies kept threatening them (Ezra 4:24). So in that same year, Darius issued an official decree that the intentions of King Cyrus before him should be carried out (Ezra 6:1) King Darius began his reign in 522 BC. History tells us so.

The difference in the 490 years predicted in verse twenty-four and the 483 years predicted in verse 25 is seven. Verse 27 explains that in the middle of that seven, the anointed one will be cut off. Jesus will preach three and one-half years, counting the number of Passover feasts he attended.

Verses 3-6

As Israel, the bride of God, is about to give birth to Jesus, a red dragon with seven heads, seven crowns, and ten horns appears in heaven. His tail sweeps away one-third of the stars and flings them to the earth. Revelation 20:2 says the dragon is the serpent, Satan.

Seven represents everywhere, heaven and earth, in a spiritual sense and literal sense. Indeed, Satan is everywhere.

Daniel had predicted in 7:19-26 that there would be four great empires, and during the fourth a terrifying beast will appear with ten horns on his head, three of which fell off. (All-inclusive power is meant by the number ten, as seen in the numbers chart.) Then an eleventh king will subdue the three kings who called themselves god. (Three represents divinity in the numbers chart.) The eleventh king will be the "Most High" (v. 22, 27). When you take three of the kings away from the ten, you have the seven remaining kings referred to in Revelation as the red dragon.

The woman gives birth, and Satan is ready to devour Jesus, but God snatches him up to him. Then the woman, Israel, flees to the desert where God takes care of her for 1260 days. This totals 3-1/2 years.

Jesus was born BC 8, according to Matthew, and BC 6 according to Quirinius' census mentioned in Luke 2:1-2. Herod the Great died between BC 4 and 5. Either way, it comes to approximately three and one-half years that Jesus was in Egypt (Matthew 2:13-23).

Verse 7-11

There is now an interruption in the story to explain Satan.

There has been war in heaven between Michael and his angels, and Satan (the dragon) and his angels. Something similar to this is referred to in Daniel 10:5, 12-13, 20-21. "But the prince of the Persian kingdom resisted me twenty-one days. Then Michael, one of the chief princes [angels], came to help me....Soon I will return to fight against the prince [angel] of Persia" (verses 13 and 20).

Jude 9 says Michael the archangel, disputed directly with Satan and won.

Then Satan (the dragon) has been hurled out of heaven. This scripture identifies who the dragon is: The ancient serpent called the devil, whose name is Satan. He was and is leading the whole world astray, so was punished, along with is own angels, his followers.

Here in verse ten, Satan is called the accuser of the brethren. As we see in Job 1:6-7, Satan still shows himself in heaven sometimes. Perhaps each time, God casts him down. Perhaps it is an on-going situation.

But Satan being the accuser sums up the whole problem of sin and death. Every time we sin, Satan is ready to pounce on us and tell God, "See there? He sinned, so now I have to kill his soul and later his body." Here we have defined the age-old problem of good versus evil. Remember, the wages of sin is death (Romans 6:23). That's a non-revocable spiritual law. God recognized it, and worked out a plan to go around the problem. The solution was that Jesus would take Satan's accusations and die in our place. Jesus said in John 12:31-32 that at his crucifixion, he will drive Satan away.

So, how do "the brethren" whom Satan accuses overcome Satan's accusations? By the blood of the Lamb. Romans 16:20 refers to crushing Satan under our feet. Hebrews 9:13-14 says we cannot get rid of our sins through the blood of sacrifices, though they did act as a substitute for our death penalty many times during the Old Testament era. Jesus finally came and offered his body and blood to Satan to take his vengeance out on.

Verse 12

THE THIRD WOE

Finally, the third woe is pronounced. Satan has been thrown down to the earth. He is full of fury, because he knows his time is short. How short? Satan has lived untold eons. He knows hell has been prepared for him and his angels (Matthew 25:41). He hates God, he hates people. So he goes around like a roaring lion, seeking people to devour (I Peter 5:8-9). God plans to stop him.

Verse 13-14

Now the interlude in the story is over (the background of Satan, the dragon), and we resume the account of the woman in the wilderness and the male child. Satan knows the power that the male child has, the potential to harm him. He must stop him and his mother. So he persecutes all Israelites (the mother) who decide to follow Jesus.

Once again, we are told that the woman flees into the desert to be taken care of a time, times, and half a time. Remember, time in the singular is symbolic of one year, times in the plural is symbolic of two years, and half a time is symbolic of half a year. So, whereas the woman and her baby are protected for three and one-half years in Egypt during his early childhood, this time they are protected three and a half years while the male child, now grown, preaches.

We know Jesus was 30 years old when he began to preach (Luke 3:23) and he preached three and a half years, counting all the Passover Feasts he attended. Though he received many death threats during his ministry, he was not afraid, but often said, "My hour has not yet come".

Verses 15-17

So Satan, the dragon, spits out water like a river and tries to drown the woman (Israelites) and her baby (Jesus). But the earth opens up and swallows the river. This reminds us of David when he wrote in Psalm 18:4, 16-19 that God brought him out of the flood, a time of emotional turmoil for him.

But there is another type of flood, the flood of baptism. Romans 6:2-4 explains that we die spiritually, and are buried in the floodwaters of baptism. But we don't stay dead. We rise up out of the floodwaters reborn to a new life. So what Satan intends as doom, turns out for the Christian to be a boon.

Still Satan continues to hate us. He begins to wage war against the rest of her offspring ~ the church that was borne out of the Israelite religion and "hold to the testimony of Jesus".

James 4:7 says we must resist the devil. Ephesians 6:10-12 says we are struggling against the schemes of the devil. When we realize that our sins are the result of giving in to Satan, perhaps it will help us resist. For the Christian, sins of attitude haunt us, along with sins of not doing good works we should be doing. We must resist.

God, help us. We know you love us. You are so strong. We are so weak. God, help us. We are drowning in our own sins.

Chapter 13. ...At a Time of God-Kings & Paganism as Predicted

DURING THE TIME OF ROME AS PREDICTED

What we see now is another interlude in the story of Jesus' birth and ministry to explain his opposition.

Verse 1

Here comes another beast, this one out of the sea of spiritual death, the sea representing all nations of the world (Revelation 17:15).

He is also with ten horns, seven heads, and ten crowns. Instead of the crowns being on the heads, they are on the horns. Horns, as noted before, represents power, absolute authority. Whereas with God we see the horns of sinlessness and salvation, with Satan we see the horns of sin and condemnation.

The word "beast" here in the Greek, *therion*, and can refer to any wild animal. It is used in Acts 28:5 in regard to a snake. It is used in Titus 1:12 to identify boorish people, the Cretans. This beast is not the dragon, Satan, but kings who serve Satan.

There are blasphemous names on each of the seven heads. Remember, seven represents heaven (3) plus earth (7), so refers to everywhere. Do not think, when we blaspheme ~ speak injuriously of God ~ he does not know. Each time we insult him by using his name as a swear word or exclamation, God knows. It does not matter whether we are laughing or angry when we use his name, we are not getting by with it. God knows.

Psalm 75 speaks of the arrogant wicked, "Do not lift up your horns against heaven; do not speak with outstretched neck...I will cut off the horns of all the wicked, but the horns of the righteous will be lifted up" (verses 5 and 10). Who are these blasphemous kings who appear during the Roman Empire as predicted by

Daniel (Daniel 7)?

TEN ROMAN EMPERORS

There were ten Roman emperors who declared themselves gods, or were declared gods by loyal subjects after their death. Most had temples built in their honor and their statue placed in the apse where the statues of gods were always on display for worship.

BC 27-AD 14 – Augustus Caesar
AD 14-37 – Tiberius Caesar
AD 37-41 – Gaius "Caligula" Caesar
AD 41-54 – Claudius Caesar
AD 54-68 – Nero Caesar
AD 69-79 – Flavius Titus "Vespasian" Caesar
AD 79-81 – Flavius "Titus" Vespasian Caesar
AD 81-96 – Domitian Caesar
AD 96-98 – Marcus "Neva" Caesar
AD 98-117 – Marcus Nerve "Trajan" Caesar

As explained in Daniel 8, the first beast was Babylon, the second beast Media and Persia, and the third beast, Greece. Therefore, the fourth beast is Rome. In Daniel 7:19:22, he explains that the fourth beast is the most terrifying with iron teeth and bronze claws that crush, devour and trample underfoot whatever it disdains. The ten horns have eyes and a mouth that speak boastfully.

This is the beast that wages war on the saints (Christians) until the Ancient of Days finally stops him. Indeed, the Roman government did war against Christians. A reading of the first half of *Foxe's Book of Martyrs* spells out just how cruel people were to Christians who refused to worship their gods, especially their emperors.

Verses 2-4

This beast looks like a leopard with feet of a bear and mouth of a lion. Hosea 13:7-8 speaks of chastising the Israelites for their idolatry and forgetting the true God. They were to be stalked like a lion and bear stalk their prey, then be attacked like a mother bear deprived of her cubs.

In Daniel 7:4-7, the same description is given of the fourth beast ~ leopard in verse 6, bear in verse 5, lion in verse 4, and having ten horns and most fearful in verse 7.

Who has given the crowns to these men? Satan has. He uses them for his purposes ~ to destroy Jesus Christ, and destroy Christians, the church.

One of the kings receives a fatal wound, but is healed by Satan. The world is so amazed, it follows the beast. It is during the reign of Augustus Caesar that Jesus is born (Luke 2:1), and during the reign of Tiberius Caesar that Jesus preaches (Luke 3:1).

Jesus' existence on earth definitely fatally wounds Satan's cause on earth. People everywhere follow Jesus. But after his death, people then forgot Jesus, at least outside of tiny Israel. Satan's darts of forgetfulness heal the beast so that Satan can regain his power.

Successive heads of the beast with power everywhere, became more and more cruel to Christians while the world looks on at the persecution with full approval. Oh how the world admires Satan.

The world loves power. The world loves success. The world worships power and success. The world worships Satan while it laughs and lies and cheats and steals and destroys, each person for his own power and success. Indeed, the world worships Satan and whoever Satan has brought to power and success, whoever makes the headlines.

Verses 5-6

Do not lose sight that we are seeing what else happens at the birth of Christ and the birth of the church. Satan is furious. He had tried to kill Jesus through Herod, but it hadn't worked. He now tries to silence Jesus during his ministry.

The citizens of the kingdoms of the beast are proud and

boastful. They hate Jesus. Jesus is trying to change everything. He calls for peace when world leaders want war to expand their kingdoms. He calls for loving your enemies when normal citizens vie for position in their own little realms so they can be admired. They backbite and condemn anyone who gets in their way.

How long does the beast have authority? Forty-two months This is three and one-half years, the time of Jesus' ministry on earth at the age of thirty to thirty-three.

And so, each person in their own way blasphemes God. The God of love, life, truth, hope, mercy, salvation from hell. Oh, how they hate Jesus.

Verses 7-8

As the followers of Jesus grow, so does the opposition. Jesus is not liked. His followers are not liked. They're too goody-goody. They're too uppity. They're too holier than thou. They don't know how to have fun. They don't know what it takes to get ahead. They let people trample all over them. Christians are losers. Oh how Jesus and his followers are hated. More and more they are hated. Satan makes sure it is this way.

And so, Jesus' enemies and the enemies of his followers bow down in obeisance to Satan, and Satan gloats. He plans to take them to hell with him. Oh, how he hates his followers.

It is this way in tiny Israel because it is the central headquarters of the Jewish religion. Proselytes from throughout the world come here. They know what is going on. They talk about it when they return to their homelands. They hope the Jesus movement doesn't spread to their country. They're confident it will never be allowed.

Those who oppose Jesus and Christianity are not listed in the Lamb's Book of Life. God knows what is going on. He has his lists, and he is omitting those who hate him. The Book lists the saved from the foundations of the world. Yes, Jesus' work of salvation is retroactive (Hebrews 9:15). The blood he is about to shed will wash away the sins of the faithful from the beginning of the world.

Verses 9-10

God always treats people the way they treat him. If we don't have time for God, he doesn't have time for us. If we don't like God's rules for life, he doesn't like our rules for life. If we don't want to listen to God, he doesn't want to listen to us.

Psalm 9:15-16 says the wicked are ensnared by the work of their own hands. Psalm 10:2 says the arrogant wicked are aught in the schemes they devise. Psalm 37:14-15 says by people's own swords they will pierce their own hearts. Psalm 140:9 says people bring trouble down on themselves by words their own lips uttered. Proverbs 3:34 says God mocks proud mockers. Proverbs 6:27 warns that people cannot put fire in their lap without burning themselves. Proverbs 26:27 says people who dig a pit fall into it themselves, and people who roll stones at others are hurt when the stones roll back onto them. Isaiah 33:1 says destroyers are destroyed and traitors are betrayed. Isaiah 59:18 says people are repaid according to the wrath they have expressed. Ezekiel 7:8 says we are judged according to our own conduct and judgments. Obadiah 1:15 says our deeds return upon our own head.

Yes, revenge may not happen right now in the midst of persecution, but it will happen someday. Be patient.

DURING THE TIME OF PAGANISM'S HEIGHT AS PREDICTED

Verses 11-13

The interlude in the story of Jesus' birth and ministry continues so we can understand his enemies.

Whereas the first beast is political, this one is religious. People who follow Satan are following the church of Satan, they are worshiping him. So, this "religious" beast speaks like Satan. This is why this second beast speaks like the dragon, Satan. He is in disguise as a two-horned lamb, but he is not the Lamb of God. He can never be.

The second beast (religion) has authority over the first beast (politics). How can this be? Actually, during this era of the world, every country has its patron god, the one their leader (general, king, etc.) declares is the one who helps them conquer enemies and remain strong. Because of this, the priests of that god, that religion, are looked to for advice, and wield power by threatening the wrath of their god on people if they do not do what the god (the priests) says. Especially powerful is the high priest. Sometimes a country is ruled by a king, and sometimes by a high priest. Occasionally a country is ruled by a priest-king.

Of course, to maintain power, the priests of pagan religions have to perform a miracle now and then. Fire plays an important part in pagan religions. Vulcan, son of Zeus and husband of Aphrodite, was the god of fire. Phaethon, son of Helios, drove his father's sun chariot and was struck down by Zeus before he set the world on fire. Faunus was from a place where thunderbolts fall from heaven, brought relics of divine fire to kindle the pyre of the heroic dead. Neptune, when angry, hurled bolts of lightning from the sky. Baal was supposed to bring fire down from heaven on sacrifices to him (I Kings 18:25-26).

Verses 14-17

Because the second beast can perform miracles and the first beast cannot, politicians rely on religion to back them up so they can maintain their power. In fact, the priests sometimes order the people to erect an image of their ruler so they can worship him. Then the priests become the priests of the ruler, and even more powerful.

When the Caesars spoke, they claimed they were speaking as a god. Nero Caesar declared he was of a miraculous and divine birth and erected the colossus of the sun god with his own facial features. The last words of Vespasian Caesar were "I think I'm turning into a god".

After the death of Domitian Caesar in AD 96 (about the time Revelation was written), his army and the senate deified him. After the death of Nerva Caesar in AD 108, his successor deified him.

The priests of every country always had enormous power.

In some areas where there was opposition to a political god, people were tattooed with a mark on their forehead or hand so they could get jobs and buy and sell in the market. Those without it were black listed. This is an important point, for such markings are referred to throughout Revelation.

In countries where "church and state" mix, with the government selecting the official religion of the country, those governments have authority to fine, imprison, and even execute people who go against the officially selected government religion. That is why so many people were imprisoned, then executed by burning at the stake and other means reported in *Foxe's Book of Martyrs*.

Verse 18

Now we begin talking numbers. It begins here and continues on into the next chapter. Numbers have meaning. The beast's true identity is given. It is not six times six times six (6 X 6 X 6). Nor is it six plus six plus six (6 + 6 + 6). It is six repeated three times for emphasis.

Remember seven represents being everywhere, both in heaven and on earth. (See the numbers chart.) Only deity can be everywhere at once, including both heaven and earth. Six falls short of heaven. Romans 3:23 says all have sinned and fallen short of the glory of God.

The number six is repeated three times. Three represents deity with God the Father, God the Word, and God the Spirit. Six being repeated three times is its effort to be God. But he falls short. The beast is not God and never will be God.

In the days of the Roman Caesars, belonging to the imperial cult was a test of loyalty to one's country. Loyal citizens were expected to make periodic offerings of incense, and received a certificate whenever they made such an offering. Christians, of course, refused to worship the emperor. The sacrifices to the emperor were used as a law-enforcement tool to ferret them out.

But the beast is not just a single entity. The beast is everyone who makes people look up to them in a godlike fashion, whether it be politicians, religious leaders, or abusive family members who demand full control. In their effort to be godlike, they condemn themselves, and their names are not written in the Lamb's Book of Life.

    This is great assurance to Christians being persecuted by pagans in the first few centuries. It is still great assurance today, as our brothers and sisters in Christ face persecution in China, the Middle East, parts of Africa, parts of India, North Korea, Russia and many other parts of the world. Even in countries with so-called freedom of religion.

Chapter 14. Jesus' Ministry on Earth

Verse 1

The interlude is over. Jesus' enemies have been identified. Jesus has work to do. Much work. After all, Jesus is the Lamb of God. John the Baptist announced him to the world that way (John 1:29). He has millions to save from Satan and his hell. He has the world to save from Satan and his hell. Oh, how he loves the world. He wants everyone to be in the family of God. He wants to protect everyone.

Jesus stands on Mount Zion. I Chronicles 11:4-5 identifies it as Jebus, Jerusalem, the Fortress of Zion, the City of David. The temple was built on Mount Moriah in the land of a Jebusite (II Chronicles 3:1). It is the same mount on which Abraham took Isaac to sacrifice to God. When asked by Isaac where the lamb was for the sacrifice, Abraham had replied, "God will provide the lamb" (Genesis 22:1-2, 7-8). Now, once again, God is providing the Lamb.

Who are the 144,000 with Jesus who have his name and the Father's name written on their foreheads, not the name of false gods? Look at the chart on numbers. Twelve is represented in the Old Testament era as the saved under the leadership of the Twelve Tribes (sons) of Israel. Twelve is represented in the New Testament era as the saved under the leadership of the Twelve Apostles. Twelve times twelve is 144.

Why the thousand? Again, the numbers chart shows that ten represents all-inclusiveness. One thousand is ten times ten times ten (10 X 10 X 10). So, symbolically, it represents all-inclusive saved ones, times all-inclusive saved ones, times all-inclusive saved ones. No one is going to be left out! God makes sure of that.

Verses 2-3

John hears voices from heaven. Their sound is like waters. The voices are not literal water; they just sound like that. Their sound is like thunder. The voices are not literal thunder; they just sound like that. Their sound is like harps. The voices are not literal harps; they just sound like that. Ephesians 5:19 says we are to sing, and "play" (*psalo*) on the strings of our heart.

Then comes a 144,000-voice choir. This is the song of those who have been redeemed. It is impossible for anyone but the saved to learn the song because they do not catch on. They do not understand the mystery of salvation from hell. They prefer to worship Satan because they do not understand God, nor do they want to. God ruins their fun.

Why does God love singing? Why does God tell us to sing? In singing we talk to each other (Ephesians 5:19). Sometimes we sing our own words (hymns and spiritual songs) and sometimes we sing God's words (psalms). And it's all to each other and in cooperative praise to him.

Why else sing? Because we can be in harmony even with people we are mad at. Harmony has the power to melt away animosity and renew love. Even when the song leader drags the song, we can express our willingness to follow and encourage each other, warts and all.

Singing is a great healer, a great encourager, a great uplifter. It is our love song.

Verse 4

The saved are those who have not defiled themselves with women. The symbolism is female because God identifies himself as our husband all through Hosea. When we defile ourselves in this sense, we are committing spiritual adultery.

Jeremiah 3:8-9 refers to people committing adultery with gods of stone and wood. Ezekiel 23:37 refers to omitting adultery with idols. Today in our modern world, we have gods of money, food, power, beauty. Some people create hobbies that are their god. Some people use a job or children or other family members as their excuse not to worship God. When we put them before worshiping God, if God genuinely loves us and sees potential in us, he may take our excuses, our gods, away from us.

We have kept ourselves pure because we are the bride of Christ (II Corinthians 11:2). We are so in love, nothing keeps us from him. We follow him wherever he goes. Where does Jesus go on earth? He goes out to seek and save the lost (Luke 19:10). Are we being loyal to our husband? Are we going where he would go?

Jesus has plans. The wages of sin is death (Romans 6:23). Jesus plans to pay those wages with his blood.

Leviticus 23:9-14 explains that the first fruits of crops and herds were to be sacrificed to God. Exodus 13:1213 says that the first child of each family was to be dedicated to God and then redeemed by paying a sum of money to the priest. Christians of the first century were the first fruits of the church, and many of these first fruits were sacrificed on the altar of the world for their loyalty to Jesus.

Verse 5

None of the saved lies. That is a dynamic statement since it is so easy to lie. Even good people lie sometimes just to get along in the world. Jesus never lied (Hebrews 4:15). Sometimes it made people mad at him, but he was willing to take it for the sake of not sinning, not lying.

The word here for "lie" is *dolos* meaning guile. In this case, guile refers to baiting people, misleading people. Proverbs 6:12-14 warns we can lie with winks, movements of our feet, signals from our hands, etc.

Lying is serious. Satan is the father of liars (John 8:44). Revelation 21:27 says liars go to hell.

But certainly among all who are saved there are some who lie. Yes, there are. Just like there are some who neglect doing good works, and some who are impatient all the time, and some who get jealous sometimes. Jesus is about to take all lies and neglects and jealousies and every type of sin onto himself, take the blame, and pay our penalty for us.

We deserve hell. But the Lamb stands with his followers for he wants to save people from hell. He stands as a shield to take the darts of Satan for us. Such love. Such amazing love! Now we continue with Jesus' life.

THREE ANGELS OF JESUS' LIFE

Verses 6-7

Angel One reveals the ministry of Jesus, taking the gospel, the eternal gospel, the never-changing gospel to the world. Jesus himself said in John 3:16 that believing in him is why he came into the world ~ so we could see the Word of God in action. Jesus goes everywhere teaching. He hardly stops to rest. He has work to do, and only three and a half years in which to accomplish it. He intends to change the world.

The hour of "judgment" is here. This word in Greek is *krisis*. It is the time of crisis, for there is no more hiding what we have done. We must now stand and "face the music". Jesus said in John 12:27-31 (1) Now is the hour of judgment; (2) Now the prince of this world is driven out. But he reassures he will draw all men to him. When? At his crucifixion which will occur in the near future.

And so he preaches and warns as Noah did in his day. He rushes everywhere warning people that they could go to hell eternally if they do not enter his ark of safety. What is the ark of safety? Believing that Jesus is the Son of God, the Word of God walking among us. Believing enough that we are willing to do everything he says, and worship him.

The wise men from the Orient worshiped him (Matthew 2:11). A leper worshiped him (Matthew 8:2). The man born blind and healed worshiped him (John 9:36-38). The twelve apostles worshiped him (Matthew 14:33; Luke 24:51-52).

How did they worship him? By jumping up and down and shouting? No, they worshiped by quietly bowing down to him in deep awe and reverence. He is the King of all kings. The Lord of all lords. And is he about to take our punishment for our sins. It's all wrong. We are the ones who deserve the punishment. Jesus, how can you take the blame for all we have done?

Verse 8

Angel Two arrives and announces that Babylon has fallen. The great and mighty empire. The unconquerable empire. The empire that was never supposed to die.

"Fallen" is from the Greek word *ekpippto* and is used in Luke 17:2 for being cast into the sea with a millstone around the neck. It is used in Romans 9:6 to explain how the Word is of no effect. It is used in II Peter 3:17 regarding falling and being led astray by the wicked.

As already seen, Babylon represents the worst of what happened to the Israelites. Idolatrous Babylon had taken them captive. Babylon now represents the worst that can happen to a soul. Peter accused the sorcerer who wanted to buy the power to give the Holy Spirit as being captive to sin (Acts 8:23).

Jesus read from Isaiah when he read of himself: "The Spirit of the Lord is on me, because he has anointed me to preach good news to the poor. He has sent me to proclaim freedom for the prisoners and recovery of sight for the blind, to release the oppressed, to proclaim the year of the Lord's favor" (Isaiah 61:1-2; Luke 4:18-19). Jesus is now on earth to set people free from the bondage of sin.

Jesus tells us, "You shall know the truth, and the truth shall set you free" (John 8:32). He goes about during his ministry on earth unshackling people from each one's individual Babylon. Soon he will open the gates of our spiritual prison to set us all free. Oh, how he loves us.

Verse 8-11

Angel Three arrives and warns that, if anyone receives the mark of the beast (from evil governments and evil religions), he will drink God's cup of wrath. They are not marked for God's eternal protection, but for their government's temporary protection. They are marked for death.

In the Garden of Gethsemane, Jesus prayed to not have to drink of that cup (Matthew 26:39), but, if he was going to take our sins onto himself, he was going to have to take God's wrath onto himself.

God warns them here that, if they don't change, they will be tormented with fire. That is how they killed many of those they persecuted ~ burning them at the stake, in hot oil and in other ways. It is the boomerang effect. What we do to others, God does to us.

The warning includes the fact that their torment will last forever. Will people leave behind idolatry? How many people even believe the warning? None of them did in Noah's day. Jesus warns that people were marrying and being given in marriage in Noah's day and refused to listen. Jesus begs throughout his ministry on earth as Noah must have. He has the advantage of miracles. Most still refuse to listen. How sad. How tragic. How it breaks God's heart.

Verse 12-13

At least the persecutors of the godly will eventually be punished. It is not our job to punish them. God said "Vengeance is mine...I will repay" (Deuteronomy 32:35). We are grateful for that. This way, we can spend more time thinking on whatever is true, honorable, right, pure, good, excellent, and worthy (Philippians 4:8) and going about doing good (Acts 10:38).

As Jesus works to save everyone who will listen, it is our job to be patient. That sometimes means being patient when we are fired from our job for some Christian standard we uphold that is not popular. That sometimes means being patient when we lose family members who disown us for becoming a Christian. That means being patient when governments come to our door, falsely accuse us, imprison us, and threaten to execute us which happens today in China, the Middle East, North Africa, India, North Korea, and many other places.

But, what if we are executed? Especially in mid-life with so much living still to be done? There is something better than this. Heaven is full of wondrous things to do, and much more interesting than anything we could do here. "Blessed are the dead who die in the Lord from now on." From now on? What just happened? It hasn't happened yet. But it's about to.

Verses 14-16

Angel Four comes out of the temple and calls out to the crowned Son of Man seated on a cloud. He shouts it is time to use his sickle. It is time to reap the harvest. That is just what Jesus has told his apostles: "Do you not say 'Four months more and then the harvest'? I tell you, open your eyes and look at the fields! They are ripe for harvest. Even now the reaper draws his wages, even now he harvests the crop for eternal life" (John 4:35-36). So the Son of Man swings his sickle over the earth and harvests mankind. Now, what to do with them?

Verses 17-19

Angel Five also comes out of the temple in heaven, and he has his own sickle.

Angel Six follows him out of the temple. He is in charge of the fire below the altar. He calls out to Angel Five and tells him to harvest the grapes, for they are ripe, they are ready.

Angel Five does so, and they become the grapes of God's wrath. God is furious at Satan and those who follow him.

But there is a twist. God's wrath is not going to be poured out on sinful mankind. Instead, it is about to be poured out on his beloved Son, for he is about to become our sins incarnate (II Corinthians 5:21). Jesus is about to drink the cup of God's wrath meant for us.

Verse 20

The grapes are taken outside the city to be trampled on, and they turn to blood. Leviticus 16:2, 14-16, 27 explains that, on the Day of Atonement, the bull and goat sin offerings are to be taken outside the camp. (Later they conquer their Promised Land, build the city of Jerusalem, build a temple, and the bull and goat are taken outside the walls of Jerusalem.)

Jesus' blood is about to be shed outside the city of Jerusalem (John 19:17-18; Hebrews 13:11-14).

How much blood will be shed? It is measured. It will rise 1600 stadia, which is 180 miles (300 kilometers) high. But this is not literal, for the entire book of Revelation is symbolic. Notice, four times four is sixteen. Looking at the chart on numbers, we see the significance of four being the earth. So 16 means all the earth times all the earth. That's who Jesus will die for.

But then, more intensity is added. Remember, ten means all-inclusiveness, and 1000 is ten times ten times ten. So Jesus' blood is about to spread throughout all the earth, times all the earth, times all-inclusiveness, times all-inclusiveness, times all-inclusiveness.

And what is his blood about to do? In Revelation 7:14 and later in Revelation 22:14, Jesus' blood washes away our sins and purifies us. What a price he has to pay because we think sin is so much fun.

His love is overwhelming.

Chapter 15. Jesus' Triumphal Entry Into Jerusalem

Verses 1-2a

The "plagues" mentioned here are from the Greek word *plege*, meaning a stroke from something. It is used in Acts 16:23 regarding being flogged and receiving stripes. Its Hebrew equivalent is also thus translated in the Greek *Septuagint* regarding bruising Satan's head and the Savior's heal.

John sees a sea of glass mixed with fire. This is the sea of spiritual death. Daniel 7:3 refers to the four beasts coming out of the sea. Revelation 20:13 refers to the spiritually dead coming out of the sea.

But to the godly person it is not the end. The Israelites walked to the other side of the Red Sea safely, while the Egyptians drowned in it (Exodus 14:28-30). Paul explains that the Israelites were baptized unto Moses in that sea (I Corinthians 10:1-2). Therefore, when we die spiritually, we can be buried in the waters of baptism and come out of those waters alive spiritually (Romans 6:3-4).

The fire represents testing and refining. The Lord said in Jeremiah 23:29 "Is not my Word like a fire?". God said in Malachi 3:2-3 "But who can endure the day of his coming? And who can stand when he appears? For he is like a refiner's fire….He will purify…and purge them as gold and silver…in righteousness." Finally, Paul said in I Corinthians 3:13, "Each one's work will become clear, for the Day will declare it, because it will be revealed by fire; and the fire will test each one's work, of what sort it is."

Some versions of this verse say those victorious over the beast are standing beside the sea, and some say on the sea. Standing is from the Greek *histemmi* meaning to stand firm. Matthew 12:25 quotes Jesus as saying a house divided against itself cannot stand. When Jesus was before Pilate, he stood firm (Matthew 27:11). And we are warned in I Corinthians 10:12, "He who thinks he stands, take heed lest he fall."

These people standing on or near the sea are standing firm. No matter what the beast does to them, they do not renounce Jesus. No matter how much they are persecuted, they refuse to recant. They will not recant. They cannot recant. They stand firm, just as Jesus is about to do.

Verses 2b-3a

The victors, as a result of what Jesus is about to do, are holding harps given them by God. Remember, incense held by the twenty-four elders when they bowed down to the ground was the prayers of the saints, and the harps held by them when they bowed down to the ground were their hearts. So now, God gives them a new heart.

And they sing. They sing the song of Moses, representing the saved in the Old Testament era, and the song of the Lamb, representing the saved of the New Testament era. They sing a duet. They sing a song of unity.

Through the Lamb, they are all about to be saved by his blood. That includes Abel and Enoch, Noah and Abraham, Isaac and Jacob, Joseph and Moses, Rahab and Gideon, Barak and Samson, Jephthah and David and Samuel (Hebrews 11). Though they were great and godly, they were not perfect, they sinned. Though they lived before Jesus, they will be saved retroactively (Hebrews 9:15).

Verses 3b-4

God is called great and marvelous, just and true, and the only holy one. He is the Lord, the God Almighty, the King of the ages.

A similar song is sung at the gates of Jerusalem. They praise God with loud voices,

Blessed is the king!
Who comes in the name of the Lord!
Peace in glory in the highest!

This is reminiscent of the Psalm 24:7 and 10, written by David a thousand years earlier as prophecy:

> *Lift up your heads, O you gates;*
> *Be lifted up, you ancient doors,*
> *That the King of glory may come in....*
> *Who is he, this King of glory?*
> *The Lord Almighty ~*
> *He is the King of glory.*

Notice, the song of the Lamb says all nations will come and worship him. It is future tense.

Verses 5-7

The tabernacle was a tent of worship used by the Israelites from the time of Moses until the time of Solomon. He built a permanent temple of worship. So sometimes tabernacle and temple are used interchangeably as it is here.

The temple is opened, and out come seven angels wearing linen garments and gold sashes. This is similar to what the priests wore during the keeping of the Law of Moses (Exodus 28:39-40). Isaiah called the sash righteousness and faithfulness (11:5).

They have with them seven plagues, which are in seven bowls filled to the brim with the wrath of God toward Satan and sin. They wait for the signal to pour them out. They will pour them all out on Jesus, our substitute.

Verse 8

Smoke fills the temple. This is a holy thing. When the tent of the tabernacle was dedicated, the smoke of God's glory filled it (Exodus 40:35). When the temple was dedicated, a cloud filled the temple (II Chronicles 5:1, 13-14); it was the glory of God.

It is impossible for humans to stand within the glory of God. Why? Because he is all goodness, all purity, all might, all power, all life, all light. We cannot fully comprehend the glory of God.

Chapter 16. Jesus, the Lamb of God, Pours Out His Blood

We come now to the trial and crucifixion of Jesus. Remember, Jesus is about to take our sins onto himself. He bravely takes the blame. Then he will suffer our punishment in our place.

The King James Version translates bowls as vials. Sometimes the author translates it cups, though this is not the same word in the original Greek. This is done so because of what Jesus begs his Father in the Garden of Gethsemane: "Let this cup pass from me" (Luke 22:42). This is no calm request. Hebrews 5:7 says "During the days of Jesus' life on earth, he offered up prayers and petitions with loud cries and tears to the one who could save him from death."

Satan is pressuring him hard. Satan does not want Jesus to go through with God's plan of salvation. Satan wants people to keep going to hell. That is what would happen if no one rescued them, for the wages of sin is death (Romans 6:23) and everyone sins (Romans 3:23). Since death means separation, spiritual death means separation from God who is Life.

Things get so desperate with Jesus in the Garden of Gethsemane that God sends an angel to help him. Even with the angel there, he continues to be in anguish and continues to try to find a way out until his sweat is even dropping to the ground (Luke 22:44-45).

This chapter in Revelation recalls in spiritual terms what Jesus endured for us. Get ready to be further awed.

Verse 1

The word translated "plagues" here comes from the Greek word *plege*, meaning a stroke from something. It is used in Acts 16:23 for stripes received from flogging. Isaiah 53:5 prophesied, "By his stripes we are healed" (KJV).

We see when Jesus goes to court, and how he is beaten by the priests themselves (Mark 14:63-65). Then Pilate has him scourged (Mark 15:15). Then the soldiers getting ready to crucify Jesus later in the morning, whip him with a reed (Mark 15:16-20).

How can Jesus' stripes heal us? Isaiah 53:3-4a explains, "He was despised and rejected by men, a man of sorrows, and familiar with suffering. Like one from whom men hide their faces, he was despised, and we esteemed him not. Surely he took up our infirmities and carried our sorrows, yet we considered him stricken by God, smitten by him and afflicted."

Verse 2

Bowl 1: The next angel pours out ugly, painful sores. The word "ugly" in the Greek is *kakos* meaning evil, bad, wicked. And the Greek word for "sores" is *helkos* meaning ulcer or open sore. They are loathsome, painful, malicious sores. When Jesus is nailed to the cross, he receives four hideous open sores to his body.

Isaiah goes on to explain in 54:4b-5, "He was pierced for our [not his, but our] transgressions, he was crushed for our [not his, but our] iniquities. The punishment that brought us peace was upon him. By his wounds we are healed."

Verses 3-4

Bowl 2 is poured out onto the sea where it turns to blood like that of a dead man. This is the sea of sin and death mentioned earlier in chapter 15.

Bowl 3 is poured out and the rivers turn to blood. John 7:38 says out of Jesus will flow rivers of living water. But not yet. First, the rivers have to flow with Jesus' blood.

Jesus' blood escapes from the wounds in his hands and feet mercilessly nailed to a cross. The cross that we daily deserve. The cross which he takes in our place.

Ephesians 1:7 says we receive redemption through his blood. Romans explains that we're made just through Jesus Christ and his blood, so that God passes over our sins. Revelation demonstrates in several places that our spiritual robes are made white by being washed in the blood of the Lamb (Revelation 7:14, etc.).

Verses 5-7

Jesus takes on the punishment of the very ones who have persecuted his prophets and saints all through Old Testament times, and in the future. He takes the blame for everyone who shed the blood of the righteous. What did they do to his prophets? They flogged them chained them, stoned them, sawed them in two, speared them, refused them food and shelter (Hebrews 11:36-38). Jesus becomes these heartless people while on the cross that day.

God's judgments are just. The penalty has to be paid. The word here for "judgments" is *krisis*, and is also used in the term Day of Judgment.

Verses 8-9

Bowl 4 is poured out. It scorches and sears people with intense heat. Jesus hangs on the cross with the sun beating down on him. He has no clothing to protect him from the burning rays, and no hand to set a little shade in front of his eyes. As the sun draws the moisture out of his body, he begins to bloat as his dehydrating body searches for more water. Finally, he whispers, "I thirst" (John 19:28).

But the ones the heat is intended for just curse God because of it, and refuse to repent. Jesus becomes these people too.

Verses 10-11

Bowl 5 is poured out onto the throne of the beast, and his kingdom plunges into darkness. There are three hours of darkness while Jesus hangs on the cross for you and me (Luke 23:44-45). It is physical darkness and spiritual darkness.

There in the darkness are people gnawing their tongues in agony and cursing God because of their pain. Jesus called hell outer darkness (Matthew 8:12). Jesus told the guards and priests who arrested him, "This is your hour when darkness reigns" (Luke

22:52-53). Colossians 1:12-13 refers to the dominion of darkness for sinners.

It is the belief of the author that, during the three hours of darkness, Jesus went to hell, then broke out, something impossible for us to do. On the Day of Pentecost later, Peter said God would not abandon his soul (not his body, but his soul) in hell. It is sometimes translated Hades, but it the same word used elsewhere as hell (Acts 2:27, 31)

The conclusion is that Jesus entered hell which he did not deserve, so we could enter heaven which we do not deserve. There had always been something Jesus dreaded beyond being crucified. As painful and cruel as it was, tens of thousands of others had been crucified, many of whom were crucified on the road to a town near Nazareth when Jesus was growing up. There was more to Jesus' crucifixion than being nailed. No wonder Jesus cried out, "God! You have deserted me!". Can you imagine an existence where there is no God, no love, no sun, purity?

Verses 12-15

Bowl 6 is poured out. The Euphrates water in Babylon (the epitome of an enemy to the Jews) is held back and the river bed turns into a road for troops from the East, from Rome.

Jesus is nearly dead. The water of life has dried up (John 4:14; 7:37-38).

It creates a sense of false security to Jesus' enemies. Three evil spirits appear ~ the dragon (Satan), the beast (kings who made themselves gods), and false prophets (paganism). Three represents deity (see the chart on numbers). They think they have won and dethroned Jehovah in heaven. Nearly everyone who knew Jesus now think they've gotten rid of him for good.

But, as a thief in the night, Jesus plans to come back to life. They cannot let it happen.

Verse 16

A final battle is arranged. The battle is in Armageddon on

the mount or valley of Megiddo. It is symbolic of final tragic loss or final amazing victory, depending on whose side one is on.

Zechariah has already predicted that a Branch will remove our sins in one day (3:8-10), he will be both priest and king (6:11-13), he will arrive in Jerusalem riding on the colt of a donkey (9:9), and that he will be betrayed for thirty pieces of silver (11:11-13).

Now in chapter 12, Zechariah says Jerusalem will be attacked but will repel the enemy (vs. 1-3), God will shield Jerusalem (vs. 8-9), and people of Jerusalem will look on God whom they pierced and mourn (vs. 10-11).

Chapter 13 goes on to explain a fountain will be opened in Jerusalem (v. 1) and people will ask their Shepherd about the wounds between his arms which he received from a friend (vs. 6-7).

Finally, in chapter 14, he says the Lord will go forth and fight the battle referred to in chapter 12 (v. 3). On that day there will be darkness (v. 6). But also on that day, living waters will flow out of Jerusalem (v. 8), and then the Lord will be king of the earth (v. 9).

Verses 17-18

Bowl 7 is poured out. Out of the temple comes the declaration, "It is done". From the cross is heard the same thing. Jesus' last words are "It is finished" (John 19:30).

Then comes the earthquake with lightning, rumblings, peals of thunder. It is so great, there has never been such a great quake since man has been on earth.

At Jesus' death, the huge curtain hiding the Most Holy Place in the temple tears top to bottom, tombs break open, and the bodies of holy people are raised back to life (Matthew 27:51-53).

Then, three days later, there is another earthquake and Jesus comes back to life (Matthew 28:2-7).

Verses 19-21

The Great City is idolatrous Babylon, the city that held

captive God's people. It is split into three parts ~ one part for the dragon, one for the beast (kings), and one for the false prophet (idolatry). Their claim to deity (remember the meaning of three) is shattered.

Hailstones weighing 100 pounds each fall on people. Jesus is a stone that won't melt away, for he has been tested and found true. But hail sweeps away the fortresses of the enemies of God, and they will now no longer be able to avoid death and the grave (Isaiah 28:16-19). People on whom the hailstones fall are furious. They curse God rather than repent.

Jesus has now overcome and destroyed Death and Satan (II Timothy 1:10). Death has been swallowed up in victory (I Corinthians 15:54).

Neither death nor life,
Neither angels nor demons,
Neither the present nor the future,
Nor any powers,
Neither height nor depth,
Nor anything else in all creation
Will be able to separate us from the love of God
That is in Christ Jesus our Lord.
Romans 8:38-39

Chapter 17. Earthly Kingdoms & Paganism Now Lose their Power

Satan is livid. Both beasts are livid. They know now that they are about to lose many of their following. Forgiveness has never been in their plans. Forgiveness is hated. They had thought they were more powerful than God and could keep all sinners within their prisons. They have been proven wrong.

How dare Jesus die in their place! But it has happened. How they hate Jesus. How they hate mercy and forgiveness and love.

Verses 1-2

The word "prostitute" in Greek is *porne*, a seller of one's self. Many who were supposed to be the wife of God, have sold themselves out to Satan; they have committed spiritual adultery.

Murderers, cheaters, thieves, bribers, the unjust and greedy are counted as one with her (Isaiah 1:21). People who are promiscuous and worship the idols of false religions, fame, beauty, power are counted as one with her (Ezekiel 16:30-36). People who bow down to wooden or stone idols, and who "worship" the goddess of sex are counted as one with her (Hosea 4:12-14).

She sits on the sea, representing the spiritually dead of all nations and languages of the world (Revelation 17:15). The kings of the earth are intoxicated with the wine of her adulteries. They think they are having a wonderful time. They think life just can't get any better. They are fooling themselves.

Verse 3

The scarlet beast is sin incarnate (Isaiah 1:18), full of the names of every false religion and every sinful act in the world. The seven heads represent the seven hills of ancient Rome whose kings have and will continue to persecute Christians. They are a reminder of idolatrous Babylon who persecuted and captured the Jews.

But the scope of the beast's power is not limited to just Rome and Babylon, for the beast has ten horns representing all-inclusive kings of the world. Idolatry rides on the backs of the kings serving Satan.

Daily they blaspheme God whom they hate, just as they now hate Jesus and his Christians. Blasphemy literally means cutting, piercing, stinging.

Other translations use the word defame or shame as in I Corinthians 4:14 where Paul says he is not writing the church in Corinth to shame them. It is translated revile or insult in Matthew 27:39, describing what people did who passed by Jesus' cross on the road into Jerusalem. In Romans 14:16 it is speaking injuriously and evil of someone or something.

In all cases, kings and their people, and pagan priests and their people treat the godly in the same way they treat God ~ with shame and insults.

Verses 4-6

The woman sitting on the scarlet beast is dressed in purple and scarlet, the colors of kings and sin (Judges 8:26) and Isaiah 1:18]. She is the queen of sin. She is beautiful beyond description, all decked out in her gold, gemstones and pearls. She is drinking, possibly from a fine goblet of crystal or alabaster. It is bubbling over with sparkling abominations. How can sin be so beautiful?

On her forehead is a declaration of all that she is. It is not her declaration, for she believes herself to be ravishing. Her followers believe her to be ravishing. God sees beyond the exterior. God sees into the rebellious soul.

MYSTERY: She may be able to hide from the world that all the fulfillment of physical and so-called spiritual needs she provides is sin, but not from God. Those who follow God also recognize her for what she is.

BABYLON: The Babylon that captivates the world and captures saints in hopes of turning them away from God who is so boring and restricting. The idolatrous city holds many people and its walls are high enough to keep everyone in. When the gates are closed, no one can escape.

THE GREAT: She is egotistical. People look up to her because they, too, are egotistical. She is self-serving, and people consider that the epitome of success.

MOTHER OF HARLOTS: Whereas she is the mother of all who commit spiritual adultery with idols of stone or wealth or power or beauty, Satan is the father of liars. Only the discerning see through her lies that she is taking them to a heaven on earth that is really hell.

MOTHER OF ABOMINATIONS. The abominable is stinking, loathing, despised. How can this be said of anything so beautiful and wonderful?

Her bubbling, sparkling drink horrifies us, for she is drinking blood. It is the blood of all the godly who stand up for Jesus and the way of righteousness. She considered them weak. She becomes drunk on the blood she spills of these hated Christians. "Drunk" is from the Greek word *methuo*, meaning to soak and to soften. Job 23:16 says drunkenness makes the heart weak. The scarlet woman is the weak one.

Verses 7-8

The angel is about to explain the mystery of the scarlet woman and beast. Mystery literally means "known only to the initiate". We have secret fraternities and covens where only members know what is going on. Sin is a mystery to non-Christians. What could possibly motivate them to risk heaven? But they do not believe they are going to hell. Surely a good God will let them into heaven. As long as they don't have to associate with those godly bores there.

The first part of this passage says the beast was, is not, and will be. The last part says the beast was, is not, and yet is. It tells of a cycle. Sin has always been. But sometimes in some godly nations, it all but disappears for a while, but then it raises its ugly head again and becomes popular again. The cycle never ends.

Sin comes up out of the bottomless pit to join itself to unaware people to enslave them as idolatrous Babylon did so long ago. But sometimes a nation becomes godly and sends sin back down into the bottomless pit. It doesn't last long, for sin is always looking for a host. Sin rises again out of the pit in search of more victims to latch on to. It is never-ending.

Sinners of the world, those whose names are not in the Book of Life, will marvel at the scarlet duo. "Marvel" is from the Greek word *thaumazo* meaning to be admired. Oh, how the world does admire sin.

But one day when sin is out of the bottomless pit, it will be destroyed. The spiritual consequences of sin have now been destroyed on the cross. Some day sin itself will be cast into perdition. "Perdition" is from the Greek word *apoleia*, and refers to damnable heresies and self-destruction (II Peter 2:1-3). It is used in reference to waste in Mark 14:4. Some day sin will be thrown away like trash, and cast into hell (see verse 15).

Verses 9-10a

The seven heads represent seven hills. Ancient Rome sat on seven hills. The seven heads are seven kings of Rome. Five have fallen, one is, and the other has not yet come. Keep in mind that Revelation was written in the late 90s. See now the list of the first five Caesars of Rome after the church started:

AD 41-54 – Claudius Caesar
AD 54-68 – Nero Caesar
AD 69-79 – Vespasian Caesar
AD 79-81 – Titus Caesar
AD 81-96 – Domitian Caesar

Of these first five Caesars, the first major persecution was under Nero Caesar around AD 67. Nero wanted to build a new Rome, so burned the old city down, celebrating it by singing of the burning of Troy on his rooftop. The fire lasted nine days. Many palaces and homes of the wealthy were destroyed, and thousands burned to death. Rather than face revolt for his insanity, he blamed the Christians, then commenced to punish them for burning his city.

"Nero even refined upon cruelty, and contrived all manner of punishments for the Christians that the infernal imagination could design. In particular, he had some sewed up in skins of wild beasts, and then worried by dogs until they expired; and others dressed in shirts made stiff with wax, fixed to axletrees, and set on fire in is gardens in order to illuminate them" (*Foxe's Book of Martyrs*, Chapter 2).

Foxe indicates in his book written in the 1500s that some of those killed during that time were Erastus of Corinth, Aristarchus of Macedonia, and Trophimus of Ephesus, all companions of the apostle Paul. He also executed Ananias of Damascus who had converted Paul, and Joseph Barsabas, a later apostle.

The second major persecution was under Domitian Caesar around AD 81. First he killed his brother, then some Roman senators to get their estates. Then he commanded everyone who had descended from David (which would include Jesus' family members) be put to death.

"The apostle John was boiled in oil, and afterward banished to Patmos....A law was made that no Christian, once brought before the tribunal, should be exempt from punishment without renouncing his religion....the pagans, if famine, pestilence, or earthquakes afflicted any of the Romans provinces...laid [the blame] on the Christians" (*Foxe's Book of Martyrs*, Chapter 2).

If anyone wanted to get rid of a Christian they didn't like, all they had to do was take him before the magistrate for any reason who would order him to take an oath of allegiance to Caesar, the god of Rome. If they refused, or if they declared on oath their allegiance to Jesus, they were sentenced to death.

In AD 97 in Ephesus, "as the pagans were about to celebrate a feast called Catoggogian, Timothy, meeting the procession, severely reproved them for their ridiculous idolatry, which so exasperated the people that they fell upon him with their clubs, and beat him in so dreadful a manner that he expired…two days later" (*Foxe's Book of Martyrs*, Chapter 2).

Verses 10b-11

A sixth king that reigns at the time of this writing is Marcus "Nerva" Caesar in AD 96-98.

The seventh king, who has not yet come at the time of writing Revelation, is Marcus Nerva "Trajan" Caesar who reigned A 98-117. Under him was the third major persecution of Christians.

Pliny the Second wrote to Trajan complaining that there were thousands of Christians daily put to death, though they had done nothing against Roman law.

"The whole account they gave of their crime... amounted only to this ~ viz. that they were accustomed on a sated day to meet before daylight and to repeat together a set form of prayer to Christ as a God, and to bind themselves by an obligation, not indeed to commit wickedness; but on the contrary, never to commit theft, robbery or adultery, never to falsify their word, never to defraud any man. After which it was their custom to separate and reassemble to partake in a common harmless meal" (*Epistulae X.96*)

During the persecutions, Ignatius traveled under many Christian guards. But he was apprehended and arrested in Smyrna (in today's Turkey). He wrote a letter that still exists wherein he said:

"Now I begin to be a disciple. I care for nothing of visible or invisible things, so that I may but win Christ. Let fire and the cross, let the companies of wild beasts, let breaking of bones and tearing of limbs, let the grinding of the whole body, and all the malice of the devil come upon me. Be it so. Only may I win Christ Jesus" (*Ignatius' Letter to Smyrna*).

"Even when he was sentenced to be thrown to the beasts, such as the burning desire that he had to suffer, that when he heard the lions roaring, he said: "I am the wheat of Christ: I am going to be ground with the teeth of wild beasts that I may be found pure bread" (Additions to *Ignatius' Letter to Smyrna* after his death).

Verses 11-14

The beast is the eighth king who is going to be destroyed, just like all of them have, for they are not gods, but frail humans destined for sentencing on the Day of Judgment.

The ten horns are ten more kings who have not yet received their kingdom. The number ten actually represents all-inclusiveness (see the numbers chart). Therefore, they represent all future kings of the world. They will reign one hour. That is, they will reign a limited amount of time.

They all come to power with the aid of the beast. Satan brings kings to power, then the kings hand their power back to Satan. It is a never-ending cycle.

But the Lamb of God, Jesus, does not let them get by with it. God knows what they are doing. Jesus makes war with them. He already has become King over all kings. Ultimately and every time, Jesus will win. So will Christians who fight sin side by side with Jesus.

Verses 15-18

Any time the waters (not water, but the waters) are mentioned, it is referring to the sea. The prostitute mentioned at the beginning of this chapter is sitting on the waters of earthly kingdoms with all their different languages ~ the multitudes of the world.

Interestingly the ten kings (all kings after this time) will hate the prostitute, paganism that commits adultery against the one true God. But in one sense, all kings hate paganism: Some because they want to be the god; some because they do not want competition from their powerful high priests; some because they no longer believe in false gods, or even God himself. (Constantine, for example, got rid of idolatry in Rome in 313.)

But, even though kings may get rid of paganism, they still do not get rid of the beast (Satan). Satan still rules the nations of the world.

The woman, by the way, is also a city, the great city. She is called Babylon the Great in Revelation 18:1, which represents idolatry and captivity to sin, who captures and kills Christians. The consequences of sin have been conquered at the cross by the Lamb, and someday will be imprisoned in hell.

Chapter 18. Rejoice!
The Overcoming Church Is Almost Here

Verse 1

The angel illuminates. At the birth of Christ, the multitude of angels lit up the sky where the shepherds were outside of Bethlehem (Luke 2:8-9). Was it the angels who formed "the star of Bethlehem"? At Jesus' transfiguration, Jesus became as bright as the sun (Matthew 17:2-5). At Jesus' resurrection, bright angels will appear and announce that he had come back to life (Luke 24:2).

Whose spender, whose glory does he have? Actually, not his own. He is illuminated by the glory of God (Luke 2:8-9). What is God's glory? In Exodus 33:18 and 34:6, God himself explained that his glory is his compassion, mercy, patience, loving-kindness, truth, and forgiving nature, but punishing those who refuse him on behalf of those they hurt.

The glory reflected in the angel illuminates the entire earth. And he makes a glorious announcement. It has to do with what was accomplished at the cross.

Verses 2-3

Babylon has fallen! The city of idolatry and persecution of the godly! We see here that "fallen" is from the Greek word *ekpipto*, meaning falling out of effectiveness.

Babylon had been home of demons. Leviticus 17:7 says idols are demons. Deuteronomy 32:17 says the same thing. When we bow down to a statue or to popularity, power, beauty, things, we are bowing down to demons. All nations have done it and will continue to do it. The leaders set the standard. What do they worship? People of their kingdom worship the same. They commit spiritual adultery.

Babylon had also been the home of unclean spirits. Jesus healed a man with an unclean spirit in Mark 1:23. Paul in II Corinthians 6:15-17 condemns infidels and idol worshipers, those who adore idols of every kind.

Babylon had been the home of hated birds, vultures. Jeremiah 5:26-28 says men in sin are imprisoned in cages. Their cages are full of deceit practiced by the rich who have grown fat by feeding on the helpless.

The nations are made up of individual people. The kings are governments. Merchants often symbolize religion which turns a hefty profit as a lucrative business. Matthew 26:3 refers to the palace of the high priest. Acts 19:23-27 tells of the high income earned by silversmiths who made idols to represent whatever people worshiped.

Verses 4-5

Now the plea. *Come out of her, my people!* "God so loved the world, he gave his only begotten Son." Remember? *So you will not share in her sins*. Isn't Jesus giving up streets of gold in heaven and trading them for alleys of trash on earth enough to convince us? Isn't Jesus giving up a "body" that can be everywhere at once for a body that is confined to just one location enough to convince us? Isn't Jesus' death on the cross enough to convince us how dangerous it is to sin? *So you will not receive any of her plagues*, her bowls of wrath.

Yes, there is still time to repent. This is not the end of the world. There is still time. It was the plea of John the Baptist. The plea of the apostles. The plea of the early church. It is still the plea. Of loved ones ~ family members and close friends who care, really care what happens to us.

The sins of people who worship things or reputations or power piled as high as heaven, and God knows about them. It is sinful to put these things before God, before family, before loved ones and even strangers who need our help. Do not think God does not notice. He keeps track of every day we worship these things.

Verses 6-8

We who dig pits are going to be ensnared in our own pits (Psalm 9:15-16). We who scheme to get what we want are going to be caught in our own scheme (Psalm 10:2). We with weapons plunge them into our own hearts (Psalm 37:14-15). We who gossip get gossiped about (Psalm 140:9). We who mock people are mocked (Proverbs 3:34). We who play with fire get burned (Proverbs 6:27). We who throw stones get stones thrown back at us (Proverbs 26:27). We who destroy others will be destroyed, and we who turn traitor are betrayed in return (Isaiah 33:1).

God said according to what we have done, he will repay us the same way (Isaiah 59:18). God said he will judge us according to our own detestable practices (Ezekiel 7:8). God said, "As you have done, it will be done to you; your deeds will return upon your own head" (Obadiah 1:15).

Further, God will take what we acquire compulsively, what we worship, and use them to torture us. People who put things first will in eternity have only a memory of their things, and not have God. People who put reputations first will in eternity have only a memory of their reputations, and not have God. People who put fame, beauty and fortune first will in eternity have only a memory of them, and not have God. God is love. God is life. God is light. Without God, it is an eternity with no love, no life, and utter darkness.

In one day, Babylon's (idolatry's) reign will be all over. In one day, Belshazzar, son of the great Nebuchadnezzar, Emperor of the Babylonian Empire, lost it all (Daniel 5:30).

In one day the Lord will fight, there will be darkness, living water will flow from Jerusalem, and the Lord will be king over the whole earth (Zechariah 14:1, 3, 6, 8-9). Set in its context, this is a description of the day Jesus was crucified. In one day he came forth conqueror over sin and death.

Verses 9-10

Kings who selected their own patron god and ordered their people to worship it, will watch the destruction of all that the so-called god stands for. Government leaders of today who worship their political power will see it all burned to ashes. All that power. Nothing.

But they stand at a distance. They fear they will be tormented too. So, perhaps they choose another god to worship.

People who worship luxury will someday lose it all. If not here, they will lose it in one hour upon their death with nothing to take with them.

Jesus said in John 12:27-31 "Now is the hour of judgment." Will people repent or move on to another idol to worship? Jesus calls everyone to repentance, to "come out from among them" (verse 4). Who is willing? God wants us to be his child. While standing at a distance, think about it. Think long and hard about it.

Verses 11-19

Merchants of the world bewail the demise of Babylon, the great city of idolatry. Religion is big business. Check the internet for any religion or denomination you are curious about. Are they really as poor as they claim? How much of the money they beg for actually goes to the needy or illiterate or spiritually starving? How big is their staff? What are their salaries? How many millions did they pay for their building? What about satellite offices and cars and airplanes? And houses here and there?

One survey a few years ago of donors to television religious empires revealed that lower-income, rural Americans in the southern United States are among the most faithful donors. What would happen if they backed out? Would those making merchandise of the church wail, "In one hour such great wealth has been brought to ruin"?

Some make beauty or power or possessions our idol. At what cost? Do we sacrifice our family, our true friends, our self-respect, our soul on the altar of beauty, power, or possessions? If we allow those things to get in the way of our soul, will God love us enough to snatch them away from us so he can snatch us out of hell?

What would we do if our beauty, power, or possessions were taken away in one hour? Would we take a deep breath and try to rebuild it all over again? Or would we realize perhaps God wants us to go in another direction with just one God ~ him ~ and one destination ~ heaven? Could we possibly come out from under it all and repent?

Eventually, God's kingdom will overcome all kingdoms of the world. God's wealth will overcome all wealth in the world. God's true religion will overcome all idol worship in the world. Come out from among them and declare allegiance to Jesus, the Lamb who was not so weak after all.

Verses 20-23

Verse 19 begins with alas, woe is me. Verse 20 begins with rejoice. Rejoice because Jesus on the cross has destroyed the power of paganistic idolatry. Jesus on the cross has made it possible for us to come out from it, repent, and live a different kind of life with a different set of priorities. Jesus on the cross has made full pardon possible.

Yes, idolatry will continue to exist. Idolatrous people will continue to persecute Christians because they think they can get by with it. After all Christians are weak and let people run over them. But God knows what is going on, and will take from the persecutors what they most value.

So, rejoice, saints! Yes, people of God everywhere, rejoice. Rejoice apostles who endured false accusations and imprisonments and stonings and beatings and torture and terrible death. Rejoice prophets in the early church who spoke God's Word everywhere they went despite persecutions by other religions.

A mighty angel picks up a boulder the size of a millstone and throws it into the sea. Remember, the sea represents the spiritually dead of all nations and languages of the earth. Babylon, the great city of idolatry, is prominent in the sea and is suddenly destroyed.

Now silence. Silent to the godly who refuse to listen to her lies. Never again does the music, workmanship, lights in windows and people getting married to each other matter to the godly person. The godly person caught up in its lies can now come out from among them while there is time. Jesus gives us time.

Verse 24

To survive, idol worshipers have had to devour those who teach the truth about false gods and the true God. The arguments of the prophets and other saints are making too much sense. Power and riches require a lot of followers. Can't allow the followers to leave. Devour the prophets and saints. Persecute them, imprison them, execute them so they are no longer dangerous. Their blood cries out from the ground.

People through the ages have heard of martyrs. Some remember meeting one or two. A very small handful became martyrs themselves. It continues. Martyrdom of Christians in the Middle East, much of the Far East, North Africa, and scattered here and there throughout the earth.

False religions run scared when challenged. Modern idol worshipers run scared too. They have to kill their opposition: Kill their reputations, kill their possessions, kill their loved ones, kill their bodies. But ultimately they cannot get by with it. Satan tells them they are the winners. They aren't. Jesus Christ is. So, rejoice.

Chapter 19. The Bride of Christ Gets Ready for Her Wedding

Verses 1-3

A great innumerable crowd has gathered in heaven. They shout in perfect harmony as one voice. No, they do not sing. They shout.

Salvation!
Glory!
Power!
Belong to our God.

True, people of the world think everyone is going to heaven, even if they don't much like God. Even though they think they are the ones with all the glory, not God. And even though they think they are the ones with all the power, not God.

The one true God is more powerful than all the wooden or silk or diamond idols in the world. The gods had tried to outwit him in Egypt, but it didn't work. Hapi (Sobi) was the Egyptian god of the Nile; God caused the river to turn to blood (Exodus 7:20). Hekt was the Egyptian frog-headed goddess of reproduction; God caused frogs to come up out of the water and overwhelm the land (Exodus 8:6). Khephera was the Egyptian god of the dung-beetle; God caused flies to cover the whole land and ruin it (Exodus 8:24). Hathor, Ptah (Apis) and Amon were all Egyptian gods associated with cows; God caused all the cattle of Egypt to die (Exodus 9:6). Im-Hotep and Sekhmet were the Egyptian god and goddess of healing; God caused boils to break out on every person and animal (Exodus 9:9). Nut was the Egyptian goddess of the fiery sun; God caused hail and flashing lightning to fall and destroy people, animals, and plants (Exodus 9:24-26). Senehem was the Egyptian locust-headed god; God caused locusts to eat every plant in Egypt that had not already been destroyed (Exodus 10:15). Amon-Ra was the Egyptian god of the sun; God caused darkness to cover Egypt for three days (Exodus 10:23).

God made the gemstones and precious metals in the ground, and if we worship them, he and can take them away from us. God made steel and lumber and everything else that goes into a great building, and if we worship them, he can take them away from us. God made families, and if we neglect God to worship them, he can take them away from us.

Jesus judged people through his teachings (John 9:39) and at the cross (John 12:30-33; John 16:7, 11; Matthew 10:15). When we worship that which should not be worshiped, it is paganism, and we commit adultery against God (Ezekiel 16:20-37)

The artificial glory and power that we idolize here can go up in smoke in a day, in an hour, then be no more. Shall we continue to worship and commit adultery against God for these things? Every day someone is being bereft of something they worshiped besides God. The smoke of idolatry goes up forever and ever.

But who is the multitude shouting praises to God? We shall soon see.

Verses 4-5

We are back in the throne room. We have not seen the twenty-four elders since chapter 15. A lot has happened since then. Jesus, the Word of God, has come to earth miraculously, escaped death threats, grown up, preached, died on the cross, come back to life to reign as King of all kings and God of all gods, and now is inviting everyone to "Come out from among them".

The elders leave their minuscule thrones and fall down with their faces to the ground at the foot of the throne of God and worship him. There they whisper, "Amen. Hallelujah."

Then a voice comes out from the throne encouraging such praise from everyone, both great and small. Psalm 8:1-9 compares the heavens to man. We are just minuscule. But God sees us. God loves us above everything he created.

Whose is the voice? It is the voice of Jesus, for he is the Word of God that we can hear and see in whatever form he chooses, even the form of a bloody Lamb.

Verses 6-8

Now the multitude again. They shout again as one voice. Their shout is so great, it is like the roar of rushing waters and loud peals of thunder.

Hallelujah! For our Lord God Almighty reigns! Yes, people of the world. You may think you are the ones reigning, but you are not. You may be creating a god in your own image, but it is not possible. *Let us rejoice and be glad.* Yes, we shall rejoice. God protects his own. If we are injured, he heals us. If we are distraught, he comforts us. If we are killed, he brings us back to life.

For the wedding of the Lamb has come. Wedding? There's a wedding about to take place? Indeed! To the Lamb, to the Son of God, to Jesus the Christ. And his bride has made herself ready. Who is the lucky bride? What does she look like? *Fine linen, bright and clean, has been given her to wear.* Fine linen? Yes, righteous acts of the saints make up her wedding gown.

Who are the saints? Saints are the saved ~ ordinary people who are saved. Paul wrote to the saints in Rome (Romans 1:6-7), to the saints in Corinth, Greece (I Corinthians 1:2), about the saints in the province of Achaia, Greece (II Corinthians 1:1), to the saints in Ephesus, Turkey (Ephesians 1:1), to the saints in Philippi in northern Greece (Philippians 1:1), to the saints at Colossae in today's Turkey (Colossians 1:2).

Verses 9-10

The marriage to the Lamb will take place soon. Who is the bride? Ephesians 5:25-27 says the bride of Christ is the church as a single body. Who are the guests? Individual Christians. Jesus said in Matthew 9:14-15 that he is the bridegroom and his disciples the guests. Who are the disciples? Acts 11:26 said his disciples are Christians.

At this point, John is so overwhelmed that he falls at the feet of the angel to worship him. Shocked, the angel tells him to stand because he is just a servant of God like John is. It is just as bad to worship our preacher, our bishop, a televangelist. Do we accept just everything they say as "gospel"? If we do, we are worshiping them. Do we check out everything they say against the Bible? If we do, we are worshiping God, the author of the Bible.

It is not to angels God had entrusted the testimony of Jesus, but to John's brothers, the Christians. At first, the responsibility of testimony was with the apostles. Peter explained when Judas was replaced with another man, that this new man had to have accompanied Jesus everywhere and seen him after his resurrection so he could be a witness (Acts 1:21:22).

Later the apostles gave gifts of the Holy Spirit which included prophecy (I Corinthians 12:10). Peter explained that prophecy was scripture (II Peter 1:20-21). Once the scriptures were written down, there was no more need for the gift of prophecy, for it would be unfair for God to have given a new prophecy to someone and not to every Christian in the world. Today, we Christians are responsible for protecting the testimony.

Verse 11-12

The white horse is back! But he never left. He and his rider have been leading the processing through history until the resurrection of Christ (Revelation 6:2). He has led the procession through all seven seals, all seven trumpets, all seven thunders, and all seven bowls. He has been leading the way because he has always been in charge. Throughout history, Jesus has always been in charge.

The rider is called Faithful and True. He is judging and making war against sin. Notice this is present tense, not something in the past or future. Paul says, "Fight the good fight" (I Timothy 1:18). He further explains, "For though we live in the world, we do not wage war as the world does. The weapons we fight with are not the weapons of the world. On the contrary, they have divine power to demolish strongholds We demolish arguments and every pretense that sets itself up against the knowledge of God, and we take captive every thought to make it obedient to Christ" (II Corinthians 10:3-5).

Jesus' eyes are now blazing fire. In fact, someday Jesus will be "revealed from heaven in blazing fire with his powerful angels. He will punish those who do not know God and do not obey the gospel of our Lord Jesus Christ. They will be punished with everlasting destruction and shut out from the presence of the Lord and from the majesty of his power" (II Thessalonians 1:6-8).

He is wearing many crowns because, since the cross, he has been the King over all kings, and the God over all gods.

Verses 13-14

His robe has been dipped in blood. We in his army wear the same uniform as the captain of our souls (Revelation 7:14).

His name is the Word of God. Remember, the apostle John explained, "In the beginning was the Word, the Word was with God, and the Word God....And the Word became flesh and made his dwelling among us" (John 1:1, 14).

Just before Jesus' death, he had explained in John 14:17-18 and 17:7 that, after he left, he would send the Comforter, the Spirit of Truth, the Word of God. Then he explained that he would be in that Word, for he said, "I will come to you." (For more on this and other workings of the Holy Spirit, see my book, *The Holy Spirit in 365 Scriptures*.)

The armies in heaven follow Jesus on their own white horses. They are wearing fine linen, white and clean, the same clothing as the bride of Christ in verse 8. So the bride of Christ is also a warrior.

Verses 15-16

Out of Jesus' mouth comes a sharp sword with which to strike down the power of the nations. Ephesians 6:17 identifies the sword of the Spirit as the Word of God. Hebrews 4:12 identifies the Word of God as a two-edged sword.

How does the Word of God strike nations? It convicts the world of sin. Of those who do not repent and change, he treads on them in the winepress of God's fury. This is present tense. Those who misuse and abuse Christians have the wrath of God on them.

God is watching. When Christians suffer, God knows, and he knows who caused it. They are not getting by with it. They may think so and the Christians may think so, but there is only a temporary delay. Eventually, all who persecute Christians receive God's wrath for hurting his children.

On his robe and thigh is written King of kings and Lord of lords. In Genesis 24:2-3 Abraham's servant put his hand on Abraham's thigh as a promise he would get a proper wife for Isaac. In Genesis 47:29, Jacob/Israel had his son, Joseph, promise to be kind to his brothers after their father died, and Joseph put his hand on his father's thigh as the sign of his promise.

Verses 17-19

Now there is a great supper fed to the birds of the air. They are vultures and invited to eat the flesh of kings and their generals and their armies made up of all kinds of people. An angel has invited the vultures to come because the angel is certain of the outcome.

Jesus has a greater supper. In it, we are invited to eat a bite of unleavened bread, representing his body killed on the cross, and his blood spilled on the cross. It is figurative, just like the supper in this chapter is.

Who are we, the saints, fighting with Jesus? The beast (the one with crowns on his head) and the kings and their armies. They are the ones who have gathered to make war. It is their idea not to accept Jesus as their king. The beast's armies are apparently on foot and at a disadvantage, for Jesus rides a white horse and his army is likewise mounted. The armies of the Lord are far superior to the armies of the world.

Ephesians 6:12 explains, "Our struggle is not against flesh and blood, but against the rulers, against the authorities, against the powers of his dark world and against the spiritual forces of evil in the heavenly realms."

Verse 20-21

The beast, representing kings of the earth is captured. The false prophet representing idolatry is also captured.

Who is the false prophet? II Peter 2:1-3; 9-19 says he is anyone who distorts the Word of God, and is like a well without water. The false prophet is always associated with the dragon (Satan) and the other beast (kings of the earth), as explained in Revelation 16:13-14.

They are cast alive into the lake of fire to never die or get relief. What is hell like? Full of pain (Luke 16:24; Matthew 25:30), and crying (Revelation 21:4), and thirst (Luke 16:24), and starvation, and darkness (Matthew 25:30), and cold (Matthew 18:12), the smell of sulfur (Revelation 21:8), no joy (Matthew 24:51), loneliness (Matthew 22:13), and where Satan can continually remind us of our sins that took us there because we didn't want to repent (Revelation 10:12).

With their leaders gone, their followers are destroyed with the Sword of the Word of God. Their destination is saved for later. But what about the rest of the enemies of Christians and of God?

Chapter 20. Satan Loses His Power

Verse 1

An angel has a key. The significance is obvious, but let's see how else it is used in scriptures.

Eliakim, the steward of the palace, is given the key to the house of David. What he opens, no one can close; what he closes, no one can open (Isaiah 22:22). Jesus had accused experts of the Law of taking from the people the key to knowledge (Luke 11:52). Jesus had given the keys of the kingdom to his apostles (Matthew 16:19; 18:18). Jesus has the keys of Death and Hades (Revelation 1:18).

Interestingly, Revelation explains that the Fallen Star (Satan) was given the key to the bottomless pit (Revelation 9:1). It was Satan's new home after being cast out of heaven. Revelation 20:1 says an angel of God now has the key.

The bottomless pit, the abyss, is not hell. Luke 8:27 and 31 explain that it is the home of Satan and his demons. In Revelation 9:2, poisonous locusts live there, and verse 11 says King Abbadon lives there, Abbadon being the destroyer, Satan, and he comes out continually. Revelation 11:7 says the beast (Satan) is there. Revelation 17:8 says the beast (Satan) is there and someday will come out and go to his destruction.

The angel has a great chain. Jude 6 says the angels who abandoned God are kept in darkness, bound with everlasting chains awaiting the Judgment Day. II Peter 2:4 says the angels who sinned are in gloomy dungeons or chains of darkness, being held for the Day of Judgment.

Verses 2-3

The angel actually seizes Satan himself, also called the devil, the dragon, and that ancient serpent. Of course we are reminiscent of the Garden of Eden where he was incarnate in a snake to tempt Eve, his first human victim.

Satan is bound 1000 years. Remember, if all the other

numbers in Revelation are figurative, this one is too. One thousand is ten times ten times ten (10 X 10 X 10). Looking at the chart on numbers, we see that ten is all-inclusiveness. Therefore 1000 years would be all-inclusive years, times all-inclusive years, times all-inclusive years. Satan is only bound, so can do some things, but not all he did before. He cannot condemn everyone to hell, for Jesus has paid their fine. But he will never be unbound. Only at the end of eternity he will be unbound, and that means never.

Satan has been bound on the cross. Before Jesus died, there was no hope for sinners. That includes everyone, even all the godly people we read of in the Old Testament, for it only takes one sin to be a sinner (Romans 3:23). Now Satan does not have the power to take everyone to hell with him. The godly have been purchased from Satan by the blood of the Lamb.

But finally, the angel casts him into the bottomless pit and locks the door behind him. Then he seals it. In Matthew 27:66, Jesus' tomb was sealed shut, probably with extra concrete around the stone to make sure it couldn't be rolled away. Satan escapes from the bottomless pit sometimes, but he is always sent back. Satan remains bound, for his chains are everlasting (Jude 6).

Verse 4

We already know that the twelve sons of Israel and the twelve apostles sit on thrones before the great throne of God (see chapter 4). Luke 22:24, 28-30 says the apostles sit on twelve thrones and judge the twelve tribes of Israel. I Corinthians 6:1-3 says Christians will judge the angels. Revelation 3:21 says all who overcome Satan can sit with Jesus on his throne, just as Jesus sits on God's throne.

Now reference is made to Roman citizens. Beheading and other swift forms of death were meted out on condemned Roman citizens. Everyone else could be tortured to death. Roman citizens who became citizens of the kingdom of God, Christians, often gave up many privileges, especially when they didn't hide their Christianity, but openly witnessed for Jesus Christ. They refused to be tattooed on their head or hand, testifying their allegiance was to god Caesar, for their allegiance was to the only true God (Revelation 13:16-17).

They willingly gave their life, allowed themselves to be beheaded, rather than betray Jesus. So God brings them back to life, gives them thrones, and makes them judges. They reign with Christ a thousand years. Revelation 11:15 says Jesus will reign forever and ever. That's what one thousand means.

Verses 5-6

Who are the rest of the dead? They are dead spiritually. God told Adam in the Garden of Eden that the day he sinned, he would die (Genesis 2:17). We know that, after he and Eve ate from the forbidden tree, they hid from God (Genesis 3:8-11), for they had separated themselves from God who is sinless. Isaiah 59:2 says our sins separate us from God. Death means separation. Physical death is separation from the earth. Spiritual death is separation from God who is life.

Colossians 2:20 says we die with Christ. Romans 6:28 says that, if we die with Christ, we will live with him. Romans 6:2-5 says we die with Christ in baptism, are buried with him, and rise up born again to live forever. The second death has no power over them. What is the second death? Verse 14 says it is hell.

So those who have been beheaded for Christ reign with him as priests. When do we become priests? It actually happens when we become Christians, for we were purchased by the blood of the Lamb and are among every nation of the world (Revelation 5:9).

The beheaded ones are now to reign with Christ for one thousand years ~ forever.

Verse 7-10

At the end of eternity, Satan will be released from the abyss to deceive the nations. He demands battle. The battle of Gog and Magog is referred to. Magog was a province in southern Babylon, and the prince over Magog was Prince Gog (Ezekiel 38:2).

They surround the beloved city of God, the church

(Revelation 21:1-2). This is a losing battle for Satan. Satan doesn't have a chance. Satan cannot win against the fire rained down on Satan and his followers. The battle is always God's. There is no use Satan trying to fight at the end of eternity (impossible, of course), because he cannot win. God rains down fire on them. When people fight God's people, he rains down earthquakes, mountains, swords, plagues, bloodshed, rain, hailstones, and sulfur (Ezekiel 38:18-23).

Eventually, Satan is thrown into hell ~ the lake of fire and brimstone. The beast (kings) is there. The false prophet (idolatry) is there.

Verses 11-12

God's throne of white is symbolic of his sinlessness as described by David in Psalm 51:7. In Revelation 5:1 and 6, God the Father is sitting on it, God the Son (the Lamb) is standing on it.

There is no place in heaven for those who flee from God. The sinful who do not seek forgiveness flee from God their whole life. It is their choice, not God's. God continues to run after them, not wanting them to perish.

But now the spiritually dead are brought back, for they must face their judgment. So, the books are open. Notice this is plural. There is a book holding God's laments and tears (Psalm 56:8), a book of everything we have done in our life with our body (Psalm 139:16), the little book with the seven thunders of judgment in it (Revelation 10:2), and the book containing the works of the spiritually dead (Revelation 20:12).

A few years ago, there were booklets circulated among churches about standing before God on the Day of Judgment, and him recalling with us all the bad things we did in our life. Remember, there are not only sins of action, but sins of attitude (impatience, jealousy, etc.) and sins of neglect (not doing good things we should be doing). Perhaps such booklets need to be revived, updated, and circulated again.

Even if a person has forgotten some of their sins, God has them written down to remind us. God does not forget. God only forgets the sins of Christians. Hebrews 8:12-13 says of Christians, "Their sins I will remember no more".

Verses 13-14

The sea (nations of the world) gives up its dead (the spiritually dead) as explained in Revelation 17:15. Death gives up her dead. Death and Hades give up their dead. Each and every person has to stand alone before God and hear the charges against him, all recorded in the books. Each and every sin recorded. None overlooked, except, of course, Christians whose sins God does not even remember (Hebrews 8:12-13).

The book of life is checked. Are our names here? It is the book of those desiring to obey God (Psalm 40:7-8), the book where no one's sins are listed (Psalm 69:28), where God remembers our good deeds (Malachi 3:16), and is made up of God's true followers (Philippians 4:3, Revelation 3:5, and Revelation 21:27). Who goes to hell? Everyone whose names are not found in the book of life. Even those who once were in the book can be blotted out (Exodus 32:32-33).

Then death and Hades are thrown into hell. Hell is the second spiritual death. The first spiritual death is explained in Romans 6:2-4.

Chapter 21. Now the Victorious Church Begins….

Verse 1

So far we have seen the birth of Christ and how he had to flee from destruction by the dragon. We have seen his life of ministry with his two witnesses ~ prophecies about him and his miracles. We have seen his triumphal entry into Jerusalem, his trial, his death where he binds Satan, and finally his resurrection. Now it is time for his church to arrive, the New Jerusalem.

The new heaven and Jerusalem are spoken of in Isaiah 65:17-23. Jerusalem was predicted to be rebuilt someday after being burned down, and then the Israelites will not have children and plant crops in vain. Some day, this earth will be destroyed with fire (II Peter 312-13).

But Revelation is symbolic. Revelation 12:12 pronounces a woe to the earth and sea because the devil has gone to them. To the Christian there is no more sky and earth because their world becomes a spiritual world. Though a Christian lives in the world, s/he is no longer of the world. Paul explains in Romans 12:1-2 that our bodies are to be living sacrifices and we are no longer to be conformed to this world. Jesus said he was leaving his followers in the world, but he had overcome the world (John 17:13-17).

The sea no longer exists. What is the sea? Revelation 17:15 says it is the sea of sinners of all nations of the world; it is the sea of the spiritually dead.

Verses 2-3

Notice, the Holy City, the New Jerusalem is not going up to heaven. It is coming down from heaven and is beautiful. Verse 9 says the Holy City, the New Jerusalem is the bride of Christ. Ephesians 5:29-32 explains that the bride of Christ is the church. Yes, the church came to us from heaven.

Some translations refer to the dwelling of God as the tabernacle of God. Hebrews 11:9-10 says Abraham lived in tents (tabernacle means tent), looking for a city with foundations, whose builder is God. He was looking for the New Jerusalem. In a religious sense, the tabernacle was the place of worship of God, later moved to a brick temple in Jerusalem. This passage in Revelation is not talking about the temple in Jerusalem which had been destroyed over twenty-five years earlier. Jesus said, even if they destroyed the temple, it would be raised up again in three days, of course referring to his body as the temple.

Now God will truly dwell on earth in the hearts and lives of the redeemed, those bought back from Satan with the blood of the Lamb. Before, God could not do this because even the most righteous man sinned sometimes, and it only takes one sin to make someone a sinner and the property of Satan. God is complete purity. God is completely sinless. It is impossible for God to co-exist with sin. If he did, he would go out of existence, and that is impossible. Now, in God's eyes, even though we are sinners, we are forgiven sinners, and he sees us as though we had never sinned! Now, God can dwell with us.

Verse 4

God is going to wipe away all tears. This is referring to people in the church. Christians live in an evil world. We experience tragedies among loved ones, and even weep with others in the world experiencing their own tragedies. God assures us here that he is going to wipe away our tears, he is going to comfort us.

David said in Psalm 116:8 that the Lord delivered his eyes from tears. God told the Israelites, "Restrain your eyes from tears, for your work will be rewarded" (Jeremiah 31:16).

For the Christian, there is no more death. This, of course, is spiritual death. All Christians die physically. But, though spiritually dead before becoming a Christian, we can die to our sinful nature as explained in Romans 6:3-9). Then, we no longer have to face the second death which is the lake of fire, hell (see verse 8).

There is no more sorrow. Paul explains in II Corinthians 6:10

that Christians sorrow, but always rejoice. Read the whole first half of this chapter; it explains all the beatings and imprisonments and everything else endured by the apostles and others in the early church. He spells it out in I Thessalonians 4:13-18 where we are not to sorrow like those having no hope, because Jesus will take us to heaven.

God tells us through Jeremiah in 15:18-19 that we get rid of our spiritual pain with repentance. David in Psalm 116:3 speaks of the pain of death; and Peter said in Acts 2:24 that God raised Jesus up, releasing him from the pain of death.

Verses 5-7

Everything is made new for the Christian. Paul says in II Corinthians 5:17 that, in Christ, we are a new creation, and in Romans 6:2-4 he explains how to get this new life.

Jesus says, "It is done". On the cross he said, "It is finished" (John 19:30). His work of salvation had been completed on the cross when he paid Satan off with his blood. Satan had gotten his revenge. Hebrews 12:2 says Jesus is the finisher of our faith.

Now come and drink. Drink of the water of life (John 4:10-14), from the living fountain of Jesus Christ (Revelation 7:17). Jesus said, whoever thirsts for righteousness will be filled (Matthew 5:6). We can even receive living waters from the Holy Spirit (John 7:2, 37-39) and Acts 2:38 tells us how to receive the Holy Spirit.

Those standing with Jesus overcome the whole world (I John 5:4-5) and inherit the earth (Matthew 5:3-5). Which earth? The new earth. And we are allowed to become children of God, joint-heirs with Jesus Christ (Romans 8:11-17).

Verses 8-9

The second death is spelled out here: hell. Who is going? It is a surprising list.

The cowardly. God told us through Paul in II Timothy 1:7 that he did not give us a spirit of timidity, but of power. And he said in Hebrews 14:5-6 that he will never leave or forsake us, so we should not fear what people can do to us.

The unbelieving. That's not a surprise. But what is surprising is that the unbelieving can be really nice people with smiles on their face and their life full of good works. That is not enough. It only takes one sin to be a sinner. The wages of sin is death (Romans 6:23). Unless a person believes Jesus really was and is the Son of God and follows his commandments, he is an unbeliever.

The abominable. Paul told Titus (1:1-11, 16) that false teachers were abominable. That doesn't mean just false teachers of various world religions. It also means false teachers within the Christian world. They teach many things that are contradictory. They cannot all be right. James 3:1 says that teachers will receive a more severe punishment, for they lead others astray who automatically think what they say must be the truth because they naively trust them.

Murderers. This is obvious too. But do we murder people's reputations? Do we go over the speed limit or drive under the influence of anything mind-numbing, thus potentially turning our vehicle into a weapon of death?

Sexually Immoral. Back in Bible times, worshiping the god or goddess of fertility was very popular because they were worshiped by having sexual relations with the priests and priestesses. Wars were fought in defense of the gods and goddesses of fertility. We today still worship them. Only now we do not place a façade on it. We call it what it is and brag about it. Paul warned the Corinthians 5:1-6 that their bragging about having an open mind in fellowshipping a man committing adultery was wrong. They needed to deliver him to Satan by withdrawing from him so he will see how serious his act is. After all, a little leaven (one person) leavens the whole lump (congregation).

Sorcerers. The word in Greek refers to enchanters with drugs. We can enchant ourselves with drugs of alcohol, pills, dust, or even drink. Or we can invite others to be our sorcerers for us by asking about our future through the stars and other means. Acts 13:6 says sorcerers are false prophets.

Idolaters. What do we idolize? What do we spend our day

working for, or at least wanting with our whole being? If it is not related to God and the salvation of mankind, it is idolatry. People can even idolize good things such as family. If we use our family as an excuse to not worship and not do at least a few good works, God can take them from us in order to save our soul.

Liars. That includes everyone. We can tell a lie outright in order to keep satisfied the person we are talking to. Or we can lie by omission. Or we can lie with our actions. Proverbs 6:12-13 refers to people who wink with their eye, signal with their feet, motion with their fingers as being scoundrels and villains with corrupt mouths. Even liars, God? Even liars.

What happens with all these people who usually seem to be nice and smile a lot? If they do any of these things and their sins have not been washed away by the blood of the Lamb of God, they will go to hell.

Hell is the second death. This is not a physical death. It is a spiritual death. God warned Adam in the Garden of Eden that the day he sins, he will die (Genesis 2:17). He and Eve sinned, and so they died immediately. Adam physically lived several more centuries, but the day he sinned his soul died. Romans 6:2-4 explains how to go through the first spiritual death of the soul so that we do not have to go through the second spiritual death.

Verses 9-11

Here comes the angel who had had the seven plagued-filled bowls of the wrath of God. His bowls are empty now. He has happy work to do. He says, "Come!" Where to? He is about to show us the church, and it is beautiful beyond description.

What is the church? It is the bride, the wife of the Lamb, Jesus. Remember, it is descending down out of heaven, not rising up into heaven. Ephesians 5:25-33 explains that the church is the bride, the wife of Jesus Christ.

Hebrews 12:22-23 says we have come (past tense) to Mount Zion, the city of the living God, the heavenly Jerusalem. With an innumerable company of angels and the church of the first-born whose names are written in heaven (Revelation 20:12, 15).

The church shines with the glory of God. What is the glory of God? It is God's goodness. Read Exodus 33:18; 34:5-6 where God shows Moses his glory. The church is brilliant. Jesus said we are the light of the world (Matthew 5:14). We are like jasper, clear as crystal. We are clear. We are pure. Jesus promised in his Beatitudes the pure in heart would see God (Matthew 5:8).

Verses 12-21

Some versions refer to the church as she. The gates of pearl are named after the twelve tribes of Israel. Mankind went through the era of Judaism to enter the era of the church.

The walls have foundation stones named after the apostles. Ephesians 2:19-22 refers to the apostles as being the foundation of the church.

The "city" is 1,000 furlongs high, wide, and deep. How many miles that is does not matter. What matters is the number. Since 10 represents all-inclusiveness, then 10X10X10 intensifies it. All-inclusive saved times all-inclusive saved times all-inclusive saved will be with the city. None of the saved will be left out. How reassuring!

Jasper can be red, yellow, brown or green, but usually is red. The church is protected by the blood of the Lamb, Jesus Christ. The city itself is pure gold. It is valuable because we were bought by the blood of Christ.

Once again the foundations are mentioned, except this time the different gemstones are named. The foundation of the church was the apostles who spent their entire precious lives for Jesus and trying to bring people of all nations into the safety of the church.

The gates are a single pearl, and the street (not streets, plural) is of gold transparent like glass. Jesus warned that the gate into the city was narrow (Matthew 7:14).

Are these also literal descriptions of heaven? Could be in some sense, as we will have spiritual bodies (I Corinthians 15:44). But they are also symbolic.

Verses 22-23

There is no more need of a temple now, because we are in the actual presence of the Lord God Almighty and the Lamb. Now Jesus, God the Son, dwells in us (Ephesians 3:17) and God the Father dwells in us (I John 4:15).

Hebrews 10:19-20 says Jesus became the curtain hiding the Most Holy Place from us, the place where the Ark of the Covenant (mercy seat) of God sat. At Jesus' death, the literal curtain in the literal temple in Jerusalem was torn top to bottom (Mark 15:38). It was 15 feet high (Exodus 26:15, 133). Now we are before the actual mercy seat of God, for Jesus has opened the curtain for us.

There is no sun or moon because God the Father and God the Son are the light. Jesus said "I am the light of the world" (John 8:12). John said in I John 2:8 true light is shining now.

Verses 24-27

The nations and kings bring their honor into it. Some translations have this present tense and some have it future tense. But for sure it is not past tense. This is what is going on right now. The cream of the crop of each nation comes into the church. The light of each nation comes into the church.

The gates are never shut. We know after the Day of Judgment, there will be no one else entering the church or entering heaven. This scripture is in the present tense. It is going on right now.

There is no night, because we Christians are not of the night (I Thessalonians 5:5), for we are the light of the world (Matthew 5:14), candles lit by the flaming love of Jesus Christ.

Nothing impure will enter it. Notice, this is future tense. Only those whose names are written in the book of life can enter the church right now and in the future.

Chapter 22. Faithful Until the Groom Comes for the Wedding in Heaven

Verse 1

What is it like inside the city, inside the church? We see the river of the water of life. This river is both a who and a what. Jesus said he had living water flowing from the fountain of eternal life (John 4:10, 14). He referred to rivers of life (John 7:37-38), living fountains of water, and fountains of water (Revelation 7:17 and 21:6).

But these waters are also righteousness (Matthew 5:6), John 7:37-39), eternal life (John 4:14 and Revelation 5:26; 21:6; 22:1), and the washing by the Word (Ephesians 5:26). There is another river that is not present in the church, the river of the fire of judgment (Daniel 7:9-10).

This heavenly river is pure. Jesus promised in Matthew 5:8 that the pure in heart would see God.

Verse 2

The river flows down the middle of the street. Notice, there is only one street in the church and to the throne of God. Jesus warned that it is very narrow (Matthew 7:14).

On each side of the river and street, that is surrounding the waters of life, is the tree of life. Perhaps the tree has two trunks where a branch spanned the river and rooted itself on the other side. Or perhaps the branches span both sides. Who is the root? Romans 15:12 refers to the prophecy that Jesus is the root of Jesse. Who are the branches? John 15:5 says all who are attached to Jesus Christ are the branches.

How did the tree of life get to heaven?

Genesis 2:9 says the tree of life was in the Garden of Eden. But then Adam and Eve were forced to leave and a cherubim with flaming sword was sent to guard the entrance so they couldn't return (Genesis 3:22-twenty-four).

Luke 16:26 refers to Abraham's bosom as the place where

godly people go after death. It is separate from the place where ungodly people go after death. Jesus told the thief on the cross he would be with him in paradise that day (Luke 23:43), and we put two and two together to conclude that the place where Abraham was the same place Jesus went.

But then Ephesians 4:8-10 says he will descend, and then he will ascend leading captivity captive. We have already seen that the captive are sinners, and we have seen that everyone is a sinner. Ephesians is quoting from Psalm 68:17-20, so this prophecy has been fulfilled. Psalm 146:7 says spiritual prisoners are set free by the Lord, and Jesus said in Luke 4:18-21 that he was fulfilling the prophecy of Isaiah by proclaiming liberty to the captives.

So, who was in paradise? The saved of everyone before the church started. That includes the thief on the cross who went to paradise before Jesus came back to life and started the church. Hebrews 9:15 says Jesus died as a ransom to set people free from Satan who took us captive the first time we sinned in Eden and on through the Old Testament. Romans 3:25 says God was patient and left unpunished those sins committed before Jesus' death and resurrection.

Who was the ransom paid to? Satan. The day mankind sinned, he had our souls. He basically told God, "You want them back? Pay the ransom. I demand the death of God." So, the Word was God…and the Word became flesh and dwelt among us (John 1:1, 14) and paid the ransom.

Hebrews 10:5 says, Therefore, when Christ came into the world, he said: "[Animal] sacrifice and offering you did not desire, But a body you prepared for me….Then I said, 'Here I am—it is written about me in the scroll— I have come to do your will, my God.'" The blood ransom was paid by God's blood (Acts 20:28).

In this passage in Ephesians 4:8-10, it says Jesus ascended, leading captivity captive and gave gifts to men. Romans 6:23 says the free gift of God is salvation. We could not pay the steep price. Jesus paid it, then passed it on to us free of charge.

Revelation 2:7 says the saved eat from the tree of life that is in the paradise of God. Revelation 22:14 and 19 refers to the river of life coming out from the throne of God and the Lamb. Paul said in II Corinthians 5:8 and Philippians 1:23 that he wanted to go home to be with the Lord. He did not mention a waiting place; he mentioned going directly to the Lord.

The tree of life is in heaven. It bears twelve crops of fruit, one every month of the twelve months. So here, again we see twelve times twelve ~ 144. What are the fruits? Galatians 5:22 says the fruit is love, joy, peace, longsuffering, kindness, goodness, faithfulness, gentleness, and self-control.

Now we come to the leaves. It is a fulfillment of the prophecy in Ezekiel 47:1 and 12 that a river of water will flow from the threshold of the temple and will grow fruit for eating and leaves for medicine. The leaves of the tree, leaves that are always produced after the fruit, heals the nations.

Jesus said he was a physician for the lost (Matthew 9:12) to heal the brokenhearted (Luke 4:18). And Peter quotes Isaiah, "By his stripes we are healed" (I Peter 2:24).

Verses 3-5

There is no more curse. What is the curse? Galatians 3:10-14 says everyone is cursed who does not do everything in the Law of Moses. It had over 600 regulations in it! No one could keep all of it. But he also said that Jesus nailed the law to the cross (Colossians 2:12-15), thus disarming it.

Instead, we will see God's face. Numbers 6:24-25 refers to God shining his face upon us. David in Psalm13:1 asked God how long he was going to hide his face from him, but later said he will see God face to face (Psalm 17:15). II Corinthians 4:6 says the light of the knowledge of the glory of God was in the face of Christ. Jesus promised the pure in heart will see God (Matthew 5:8). I John 3:2 says we shall see him as he is.

God's name will be on our forehead. The Jewish high priest wore the words "Holiness to the Lord" on his forehead. An expanded study of the mark on the forehead is in chapter seven.

There is no night in the church for God gives us our light, as explained in chapter 21. We shall reign forever. This is future tense, but Revelation 1:6 says it is present tense. We are priests and kings reigning and serving now and forever.

Verses 6-11

Now we look forward to the end of the world. The angel tells John everything he has shown him are from the same God who inspired the ancient prophets. But there is more.

Jesus speaks. He will speak four times in this chapter. The first time he speaks he announces two things: He is coming quickly, and the words John has written about his vision are prophecy.

But John falls down at the feet of the angel. Don't we sometimes "worship" the messengers who bring us the gospel? Preachers, bishops and others? We are not to do that. Worship what God says directly to us in his Bible, but never the messenger.

Then the angel warns again that the time is near, so John must spread the word among the brethren what he has seen and heard.

Jesus has done what he could to save mankind. But sinners continue to sin, some of them coming to God for forgiveness. So be it. Jesus has done all he could. The rest is up to us.

Verses 12-15

Now Jesus speaks a second time. He repeats what he just said before and what the angel just told John. Jesus is coming soon. This time he adds a message to Christians. He is bringing his reward with him, based on our works. Our salvation is not based on works, but our salvation will be proven to the world by our works, in our effort to save more people of the world.

Then another warning: Only those who have washed in the blood of the Lamb have a right to the tree of eternal life and can enter the city, the church. Jesus begs the world to come to him for safety, but they laugh on.

Who is outside the city? He calls them dogs: Everyone who practices sorcery, who are sexually immoral, who murder, who commit idolatry against God by worshiping other things, and liars.

There it is again. Even liars are kept out of the city of God, the church, unless we ask forgiveness and try not to lie.

Verses 16-17

Jesus speaks again. He reminds John (and us) that he is the prophesied root of Jesse, descendant of King David. Perhaps that brings back a familiar memory to John, for while Jesus was on earth, John was Jesus' cousin, their mothers (Mary and Salome) being sisters. That was so long ago. So long ago. Now John is a very old man. Now Jesus is eternal.

Then John is reminded of Jesus' majesty. Though Jesus has inherited David's throne, his is an eternal throne with an eternal kingdom. And, Jesus is the bright Morning Star, not Satan who claimed to be the morning star in Isaiah 14:12. Satan is the fallen star. Yes, Jesus brings morning to everyone who believes in him and follows his commandments. How he longs to bring it to everyone. How he loves everyone. His love never dies. His love is eternal.

Verses 18-21

Now it is our turn to speak. The Holy Spirit is with us here on earth (John 14:17 and Acts 2:38). The Holy Spirit is the Comforter Jesus sent to us. (See also my book on this subject called *The Holy Spirit in 365 Scriptures*.) The bride of Christ, the church, inspired by the Holy Spirit on earth tells Jesus, "Come!"

The bride and Spirit then turn to the world and say, "Come!" Everyone who is so very spiritually thirsty and does not understand why, come! Everyone with empty days and years, come! Everyone who wonders what life is all about, come!

John's vision is now gone. He has written everything he remembers in a book. He is back on the Isle of Patmos and will die soon (Revelation 1:9).

Often he remembers back when Jesus had first approached him. No, not as a fisherman so long ago in their youth, but the moment he had approached him on the sands of the island just before the vision began. So many years after Jesus' ascension into heaven, he had heard the familiar voice once again. Oh, it had been thundering and sounded like a trumpet, but he would know that voice anywhere. That familiar voice (Revelation 1:10).

When he had turned and seen him in his heavenly wonder, John had fallen to his face and worshiped him. He had trembled in fear. Was Jesus angry at something? Had he done something wrong? Had he failed him? How John remembers what Jesus had done next. His old friend, his savior, the creator of the world had touched him. It had been so long since he had felt Jesus' touch (Revelation 1:12-13)

His thoughts turn back to his book. Now it is the end of his written account about the vision that had followed Jesus' appearance. The vision must be protected. The words must be protected. At all costs, protected. John warns that, if anyone adds anything to the words of this book, God will add the plagues described in it. If anyone takes out any of the words of this book, their share in the holy city, the church, will be taken away. No one is to tamper with the Word of God.

One last time, we hear Jesus. He is still saying "Come". And he is promising to come to us quickly. Oh how we need Jesus to come quickly. Life around us is broken and shattered and we don't know how to fix it. There is selfishness and greed and lies and envy and worshiping artificial things all around us. We need to get away from it all. Sometimes we grow weary. "Why do you wait so long?" we ask Jesus.

He will come. He will come at the end of our life, and that will be soon enough.

Amen. So be it. Everything in this book. Amen. Your promise, Jesus. Amen.

Grace. Our last blessing. Graciousness, spiritual pleasure, thanksgiving be with all of us. Not just part of us, but all. All who read and are amazed. We whisper, amen, and fall to our faces in worship.

Come to me,

All you who are weary and burdened,
And I will give you rest.
Take my yoke upon you
And learn from me.
For I am gentle
And humble in heart
And you will find rest
For your souls.

Matthew 11:28f

SYNOPSES OF EACH CHAPTER
(Does not include chapters 1-3 of Revelation)

Synopsis 4: GOD'S THRONE ROOM:

Around the throne of God are representatives of God's saved people in the Old Testament and the New Testament. They are clothed in sinlessness and crowned with eternal life.

The Spirit of God is in heaven as well as on earth, and reveals our true value with the refiner's fire of his Word ~ either condemning or saving us. In front of the throne of God is a sea of death and resurrection (baptism) of the saved.

In the middle of and around the throne of God are earth-like living beings that can see everywhere and go everywhere. They represent God through Jesus coming to earth as our king, priest, prophet, and as a man who offered his body to die in our place for our sins.

Synopsis 5: JESUS IS INTRODUCED:

God on his throne holds his book telling about the sinfulness of mankind and the possibility of forgiveness of those sins. An angel claims no one can open the Book of Sin and Salvation, so John weeps. But the saved shout out, "The root of David can!".

In the middle of the throne of God, the Son stands ready for action. He shows how he will become the sacrificial Lamb of God, so takes the Book of Sin and Salvation.

The saved, holding their hearts and prayers close, sing praises right to Jesus. When our souls are up for bid, Jesus will be willing to pay the highest needful price ~ his human blood.

Now the angels understand, and join the throng so large we cannot count them, and shout praises about the Lamb. And finally, even the lost join the throng and praise the Lamb. They end the celebration with a quiet amen, and worship God.

Synopsis 6: SIX SEALS OF SIN IN THE BOOK OF HISTORY:

Six seals of sin in the Book of Sin and Salvation are opened to a historical procession. (1) At the head is a perfect conquering king ~ Jesus ~ leading the way to slay evil and death. (2) Behind him is a warrior who conquers Israel for continually sinning and failing to be sinless ~ not getting it right. (3) Behind him is famine that starves Judah into submission, and plague that kills the rest of Judah for failing to be sinless ~ not getting it right. (4) Behind him is Death that goes after pagan nations because they too fail to be sinless ~ to get it right. (5) Behind him are martyred prophets who tried to warn Israel, Judah and the pagans who couldn't be sinless ~ couldn't get it right.

How can the problem of sin be solved? (6) Jesus can be crucified to pay the death penalty. There the sun becomes black, the moon turns to blood, and there is an earthquake. Then Satan's power fails. The Day of Decision arrives for everyone to choose between good and evil. Heaven opens, and Jesus is received, while sinners prefer to hide from God rather than believe.

Synopsis 7: SEVENTH SEAL IS SALVATION.

But, before Jesus opens the seventh Seal of Salvation ~ the Great Seal of the living God ~ he checks to see who will be saved. Many Israelites in past history failed to be perfect; they kept sinning. But God offers forgiveness to, not only the Israelite tributes, but sinners of all nations, including us today. Jesus' blood retroactively and completely washes away, not only the sins of Israelites who had the Law of Moses, but the sins of all other nations who did not have the Law of Moses ~ both of which failed to be sinless. Everyone waves palm branches in gratitude.

Even other nations during the era of the Old Testament have a chance at salvation. The big difference is that they endure tribulation, persecution, by their countrymen who are pagans. Life is not easy for believers living in pagan lands. But, now they serve him and the Lamb day and night. No more running for their lives and suffering hunger, thirst, and the burning sun. Now God wipes away their tears.

Synopsis 8: GOD PUNISHES THE PUNISHERS:

God has kept silent about his plans for salvation except for the periods when his prophets warned people not to sin, and promised a future liberation from sin.

Then he gives reminders of how he always punished the punishers of his people in the past. The trumpet blasts of war sound before battle. He punished Egypt for enslaving the Israelites, Tyre for taking advantage of them when Jerusalem was destroyed, Babylon and Assyria for enslaving his people, and the Babylonian king for declaring himself God. He made them drink the waters of bitterness. He promises to keep on punishing the punishers of Christians even today.

Synopsis 9: ISRAELITES PUNISHED:

Long ago, out of heaven fell Satan who was then given the key to his earthly kingdom. He opened the door of history, and out of it came earthly kings with powers to torment the Israelites who were sinful for half the time. They ruled the earth and worshiped idols, and committed adultery with false gods.

PUNISHERS PUNISHED: Then God said the punishers of his people would now be punished ~ the empire on the Euphrates, the Babylonians. God used the Persians with an innumerable army to punish the Babylonians.

Despite all this, people who worshiped idols still refused to repent ~ just as they do today. Also people who murdered, used witchcraft, were sexually immoral, or stole from others still refused to repent ~ just as they do today.

Synopsis 10: DAY OF JUDGMENT POSTPONED:

An angel comes reflecting the glory, blessings and leadership of God. Everyone in history has been sinful, so now is the time for the final judgment and punishment. Instead, judgment is interrupted because God is not willing for anyone to be lost. The last Trumpet to blast forth is delayed. John takes the bread of life, which is the Word of God, and prepares to tell all nations of the world. But the nations treat those words bitterly because they do not want to hear it. The postponement remains anyway.

Synopsis 11: PREDICTIONS OF JESUS' ARRIVAL THROUGH END OF THE WORLD:

The measurement of the earthly temple is minuscule compared with the real temple in heaven, which Jesus will enter when he dies in our place. Christians are also the temple of God, and he measures activities of our lives, whether or good or bad.

God knows all, and had predicted Jesus would come after the Babylonian kingdom, the Persian kingdom, the Grecian kingdom, and during the Roman kingdom. At that time, Jesus was destined to create the kingdom that will never be destroyed, his church. The king of Rome was predicted to persecute the saints half the time.

Once here, Jesus will have two witnesses that he was the Son of God: (1) His miracles from the power of the Holy Spirit, and (2) prophecies about him made by his Father in his Word. God's Word could either save or condemn people. Finally, the Romans were destined to crucify Jesus in Jerusalem. Jesus will be in his grave 3-1/2 days, but the power of his words and miracles will remain alive. His enemies will rejoice that he died. But after 3-1/2 days, his spirit will return to them. Then Jesus will ascend to heaven.

Sinners will be punished, but God is patient and continues to give everyone a chance to repent. But, eventually, on the Day of Judgment, even all sinners who are dead spiritually will fall onto their faces and worship Jesus. And the kingdom of Jesus, the church, will be taken to heaven where the true temple of God is.

Now is the time for all these predictions to be fulfilled.

Synopsis 12: JESUS' BIRTH AS PREDICTED....

Eventually, the religion of the Jews gives birth to the Christian religion during the time when Rome ruled the world. Exactly 483 years after the order was made to rebuild Jerusalem, Jesus comes and begins preaching. He ministers half of seven years; that is, 3-1/2 years. Thirty years earlier, Satan had stood ready to devour baby Jesus, but an angel sent him to Egypt for 2-1/2 more years of protection.

Satan had been cast out of heaven, but sometimes he returns to try again. There he accuses Christians, but always fails because Jesus washes our sins away with his blood. Therefore, Christians love Jesus as much as he loves us, even if we have to die defending him. God prepared hell for Satan, and Satan is so mad, he intends to take as many people there with him as possible. He persecutes believers to get them to blame God and desert God.

Satan tries to drown us in the sea of sin and death, but God's Word and God's love lifts us up through baptism from death unto rebirth, and saves us. Even today, Satan is angry and continues to make war with God's offspring, the church.

Synopsis 13: ....AT THE TIME OF GOD-KINGS, AS PREDICTED:

Jesus arrived during the time of Rome, as predicted. A dynasty of ten Roman Caesars claimed to be gods. One of the kings, Tiberius Caesar, was dead to church activities, not even noticing it, but the next king began persecuting the church. Christians who refused to burn incense to the Caesars as gods were considered traitors. They were thrown in prison and put to death, but God promised he would do the same to their persecutors some day ~ the boomerang effect.

....AT THE TIME OF PAGANISM, AS PREDICTED: Jesus also arrived during the time that paganism was at its height as predicted. Paganism made it possible for people to believe the Caesars were gods. Many other pagan gods, according to myths, brought fire down from heaven.

Paganism was so powerful, the Caesars allowed pagan priests to punish anyone not believing in the gods. But the pagans did not go unseen by Jehovah who marked them for judgment. The mark meant they fell short of God's glory and blindly followed Satan.

Synopsis 14: JESUS' MINISTRY ON EARTH:

Jesus and all the saved now stand on the mountain of the true temple of God, singing the song of redemption and the coming bride of Christ ~ the church ~ who will never worship Satan, but worship only God.

Jesus is now ready to destroy Satan's power to destroy sinners, for Jesus is about to take on the sins of the world and drink the cup of the wrath of God over sin. Then, as on the Day of Atonement in the Old Testament when the blood of the sacrificial lamb was taken outside the city, so Jesus blood will be shed outside the city of Jerusalem, and his blood will cover the sins of the entire world.

Synopsis 15: JESUS' TRIUMPHAL ENTRY INTO JERUSALEM:

Saints will be able to go into the sea of death and then be resurrected through baptism, and stand on the other side victorious. They will be able to overcome the fires of testing and not be identified with Satan. Their song will unite the saved under Moses of the Old Testament with the saved under Jesus of the New Testament.

The temple is about to be opened, and angels carrying the cup of God's wrath get ready to pour it out onto Jesus. No one can then enter the temple because God's glory is there. But soon, Jesus will enter as our high priest, and make it possible for us to enter also through him the doorway curtain that will split open at his death.

Synopsis 16: JESUS, THE LAMB OF GOD, PAYS WITH HIS BLOOD:

It had been predicted that Jesus would receive God's wrath by making him a guilt offering for our sins. **Now is the time!** Jesus' hour of judgment is during his crucifixion. He is nailed to the cross and inflicted with three excruciating nails, and his blood flows from them. At his death, both blood and water flow out of him. He is scorched by the sun and becomes thirsty. There is darkness three hours, and Satan's kingdom is judged to be the kingdom of darkness. Observers at the crucifixion blaspheme God by taunting Jesus and not believing in him. Then Jesus, who had called himself the living water, dries up and dies.

Satan thinks he has won. But it is temporary. No one expects Jesus to return to life. The battle of Megiddo fulfills Zechariah's prophecy that the heavenly Jerusalem, the true one in heaven, would be attacked, but God would shield it. Indeed, as Jesus dies, people look on the one they pierced, then mourn for his death.

At his death, Jesus says, "It is finished" and there is a great earthquake that shakes the earth. At Jesus' resurrection, God said, "It is finished." Jesus was now the cornerstone, more solid than huge hailstones that melt away. Jesus has now overcome death. Still, bad things happen to people. Doubters and atheists blaspheme God and blame him for bad instead of Satan. Ultimately all bad things are caused by Satan. But Jesus has now overcome.

Synopsis 17: EARTHLY KINGDOMS & PAGANISM NOW LOSE THEIR POWER.

Idolaters and hypocrites commit adultery against God by selling themselves to any kind of sin. They ride on the beast of sin incarnate, but see themselves as beautiful. Pagans ride on the backs of kings who order their people to worship their chosen god, or themselves as a god.

There was a Roman Caesar in John's time who was persecuting Christians, and there were destined to be two more. They have all-inclusive power, but only for a short period of time. Though they go to war against Jesus, ultimately Jesus always wins. Eventually a king was destined to come along and destroy the other kings, but Jesus will still rule in the world.

Synopsis 18: REJOICE! THE OVERCOMING CHURCH IS ALMOST HERE.

Some day an angel of God will declare that paganism has fallen with its false gods. Until then, God cries out "Come out" and repent, for God sees and knows everything we do and will punish people in false religions. Paganism will be burned to a crisp, but former worshipers will fear and still not repent Especially devastated will be the wealthy who made their money through religion. If anything of paganism is left, it will be thrown into spiritual death so far it will never be heard from again. Gone will be their beautiful music, statues, temples, and delicacies. And finally, God will fulfill his promise that someday he will bring vengeance on those who kill Christians.

Synopsis 19: THE BRIDE OF CHRIST GETS READY FOR HER WEDDING:

Everyone in heaven unites with a loud voice praising God. Jesus' death, burial and resurrection have passed judgment on paganism. Then everyone everywhere praises God. Now is the time for Jesus to create the church who is to be his bride, and his guests the individual Christians of the church rejoice.

Jesus mounts up as captain of our salvation, to take vengeance on the enemies of his people, dressed in a robe dipped in his own blood, and with the names Faithful and True. Soldiers of his army have always followed him, and their uniforms are the same as their captain's

God's Word convicts the world of sin in fulfillment of his promise to take vengeance on our enemies He casts Satan and his false prophets into hell, which is the absence of heaven. And the Bride of Christ gets ready for her wedding.

Synopsis 20: SATAN LOSES HIS POWER:

An angel from God has the key to Satan's kingdom He is always bound, but even then sometimes deceives people.

Heaven is full of the thrones of those who have been faithful to Jesus unto death and were truthful witnesses. These are they who were buried in baptism unto death (sin) and raised up with Christ, sharing in his reign.

Eventually God will fight his last battle with Satan, and God will win. Then he will cast Satan into hell where also are death and Hades. Then God will judge the lost based on the books that list their works during life, and those spiritually dead ~ all whose names are not in the Book of Life. Then sinners, the possibility of death, and the realm of the dead will be no more, for they will all be cast into hell with Satan.

Synopsis 21: NOW THE VICTORIOUS CHURCH BEGINS:

Originating in heaven is the church, presented to Jesus Christ as his bride. God the Son dwells with us and still does. After his work on earth is done, Jesus will say, "It is done."

Mankind entered the Jewish era through the twelve tribes of Israel. The twelve apostles became the foundation of the church. The church is high enough that it can hold all the saved of the Old Testament and of the New Testament eras. The wall is high enough that it can protect the saved of the Mosaic era and the saved of the Christian era.

God keeps the gates of the church open so the kings of earth can brig their true glory ~ Christians ~ into it ~ all listed in Jesus' Book of Life.

Synopsis 22: THE CHURCH REMAINS FAITHFUL UNTIL ITS GROOM COMES FOR THE WEDDING IN HEAVEN:

Living waters of life flow from the throne of God to heal the nations of their sins. In the church and also in heaven there is no need for the sun, for God is its light.

Jesus personally tells us that he is coming suddenly. Then he will give everyone according to what we have done. Jesus is the beginning and ending of everything; he is life; he is eternity. Outside of the church and heaven are unforgiven sinners who constantly ignored Jesus.

    Jesus, God born human for us, is also our bright and morning star. And so we believers reply, "COME, LORD JESUS!" After John warns us not to change anything in this book, Jesus calls out one last time, "YES! I AM COMING SOON!" Do you hear him?

Jewish Symbolic Meaning Of Numbers

#	MEANING	SCRIPTURE	EXPLANATION IN THE SCRIPTURE
1	Unity	Genesis 2:24	…cling unto his wife and they shall be one
		Numbers 14:15	…,this people as one man
		John 10:30	"I and my Father are one"
		Ephesians 4:3f	…unity of the spirit…one body
2	Strength	Ecclesiastes 4:9f	Two are better than one…if they fall, the one will lift up his fellow.
		Ecclesiastes 4:11f	If two lie together, they have heat…If one prevail…two withstand
		Song of Songs	What will you see in the Shulamite? As it were…two armies.
		Amos 3:3	Can two walk together except they be agreed?
3	Heaven	Matthew 28:19	…baptizing in the name of the Father…Son…Holy Spirit
		John 14:16f	I will pray to the Father and he shall give you…the Spirit of Truth
		I John 5:7	…three that bear record in heaven: Father, Word, Holy Spirit.
4	Earth	Daniel 11:4	…kingdom divided toward the four winds
		Matthew 24:31	They shall gather his elect from the four winds
		Revelation 4:1	…four angels on four corners holding four winds
5		NOTE	There is no scripture in the Bible using 5 figuratively. It

				could be applied to HALF of 10, all-inclusiveness.
6	Sin		See below	Falling short of 7 (7 less 1 = 6)
7	Each & every all, universal, everywhere, everything		Deuteronomy 28:7	…enemies…shall come out against you one way and flee before you seven ways.
			I Samuel 2:5	…so that the barren has born seven…children
			Psalm 12:6	The words of the Lord are pure words as silver tried in a furnace…purified seven times
			Proverbs 24:16	A just man falls seven times and rises up again.
			Luke 17:4	If he trespass against you seven times in a day…you shall forgive
			NOTE	3 (heaven) + 4 (earth) = 7
10	All		Numbers 14:22	…have tempted me now these ten times…
			I Samuel 1:8	"Am I not better to you than ten sons?
			Job 19:3	These ten times you have reproached me.
			Matthew 18:21	…forgive him…till seven times…until seventy times seven (7 x 10)
12	God's rule on Earth		Exodus 28:21	*Names of 12 sons…patriarchs…tribes of Israel*
			Matthew 10:2	*Names of the 12 apostles*
			Revelation 21:12	*Names of 12 tribes of Israel on the 12 gates into heaven*
			Revelation 21:13	*Names of the 12 apostles on the 12 foundations of heaven*
100	Intensity		Ecclesiastes 6:3	If a man beget 100 children…and his soul be not filled with good…
			Proverbs 17:10	…though a sinner does evil a hundred times…

		Mark 10:30	...receive a hundred fold now in houses...brethren...sisters...eternal life
1000	Intensity multiplied	Deuteronomy 7:9	...God, which keeps covenant...to a thousand generations
		Psalm 91:7	A thousand shall fall at your side.
		Ecclesiastes 6:6	Though he live a thousand years twice told, yet has he seen no good...
10,000	Intensity multiplied again	Psalm 3:6	I will not be afraid of ten thousands of people.
		Song of Songs 5:10	...the chiefest among ten thousand
		Daniel 7:10	Ten thousand times ten thousand stood...judgment was set and the gooks were opened.
¼	Small portion, scant	Numbers 23:10	Who can count the dust of Jacob or number the fourth of Israel
		II Kings 6:25	...fourth of a cab of [dove's] dung (KJV)

Thank You

      Thanks for reading my book! I'm honored that you chose to spend your precious time with my research. You are appreciated. I'm an independent author who relies on my readers to help spread the word about stories you enjoy. Would you take a few minutes to let your friends know on Facebook, Pinterest... wherever you go online?

      Also, each honest review at online retailers means a lot to me and helps other readers know if this is a book they might enjoy,

      I welcome contact from readers. At my website (below), you can do so. You can also sign up for my newsletter (below) to be notified of half-price books and new releases.

About the Author

Katheryn Maddox Haddad grew up in the cold north and now lives in Arizona where she does not have to shovel sunshine. She basks in 100-degree weather with palm trees, cacti, and a computer with most of the lettering worn off.

She has a bachelor's degree in English, Bible, and history, from Harding University, a Master's Degree in management and human relations from Abilene Christian University, and part of a Master's Degree in Bible from Harding University, including Greek studies.

She spends half her day writing, and the other half teaching English over the internet worldwide using the Bible as textbook through World English Institute. She has taught some 7000 Muslims, mostly in the Middle East. Students she has converted to Christianity are in hiding in Afghanistan, Iran, Iraq, Yemen, Jordan, Somalia, Sierra Leone, Uzbekistan, Tajikistan, Indonesia, and Palestine. "They are my heroes," she says.

In addition to her seventy-seven books (non-fiction, novels, and storybooks), she has written numerous articles for *Gospel Advocate, Twentieth Century Christian, Firm Foundation, Christian Bible Teacher, Christian Woman,* and several world mission publications. Her weekly column, *Little-Known Facts About the Bible,* appeared several years in newspapers in North Carolina and Texas.

Buy Your Next Book Now

CHRISTIAN LIFE
http://bit.ly/Christianlife
Applied Christianity: Handbook 500 Good Works
You Can Be a Hero Alone
Worship Changes Since 1st Century + Worship 1sr Century Way
The Best of Alexander Campbell's Millennial Harbinger
Inside the Hearts of Bible Women-Reader+Audio+Leader
The Lord's Supper: 52 Readings with Prayers

BIBLE TEXT STUDIES
Revelation: A Love Letter From God
The Holy Spirit: 592 Verses Examined
Was Jesus God? (Why Evil)
365 Life-Changing Scriptures Day by Date
Love Letters of Jesus & His Bride, Ecclesia
Christianity or Islam? The Contrast
The Road to Heaven
http://bit.ly/BibleTexts

FUN BOOKS
Bible Puzzles, Bible Song Book, Bible Numbers
http://bit.ly/BibleFun

TOUCHING GOD SERIES
365 Golden Bible Thoughts: God's Heart to Yours
365 Pearls of Wisdom: God's Soul to Yours
365 Silver-Winged Prayers: Your Spirit to God's
http://bit.ly/TouchingGodSeries

-SURVEY SERIES: EASY BIBLE WORKBOOKS
→Old Testament & New Testament Surveys
→Questions You Have Asked-Part I & II
http://bit.ly/BibleWorkbooks

HISTORICAL RESEARCH BIBLE
for Novel, Screenwriter, Documentary & Thesis Writers
http://bit.ly/32uZkHa

GENEALOGY: How to Climb Your Family Tree Without Falling Out
Volume I & 2: Beginner-Intermediate & Colonial-Medieval
http://bit.ly/GenealogyBeginner-Advanced

Connect With The Author

Website: https://inspirationsbykatheryn.com

Facebook: bit.ly/FacebooksKatherynMaddoxHaddad

Linkedin: http://bit.ly/KatherynLinkedin

Twitter: https://twitter.com/KatherynHaddad

Pinterest: https://www.pinterest.com/haddad1940/

Goodreads: https://www.goodreads.com/katherynmaddoxhaddad

Get A Free Book

Sign up for Katheryn's monthly newsletter with half-price books for the whole family and insider tips on what's coming next.
http://bit.ly/katheryn

Join My Dream Team

Members get the first peek at my newest book and have fun offering me advice sometimes. I have a point system of rewards for helping me get the word out. Check it out here:
http://bit.ly/KatherynsDreamTeam

www.ingramcontent.com/pod-product-compliance
Lightning Source LLC
Chambersburg PA
CBHW071516080526
44588CB00011B/1448